Risk Management Professional
1. Planning Risk Management
2. Identifying Risk
3. Analyzing Risk
4. Responding to Risk

1. Planning Risk Management (by PMBOK® Guide Sixth Edition)

1.1. Understanding Project Risk
1.2. Types of Project Risks
1.3. Reducing the Uncertainty of Risk
1.4. Understanding Risk Responses
1.5. Inputs to Plan Risk Management
1.6. Tools and Techniques to Plan Risk Management
1.7. The Risk Management Plan
1.8. Sample Risk Management Plan
1.9. The Risk Probability and Impact Matrix
1.10. Exercise: Planning Risk Management

1.1. Understanding Project Risk

The projects you'll manage will face many different risks. First of all, let's define what we mean by risk. Project risks have two characteristics. They're events that might happen, and they have the potential to impact one or more of the project objectives.

There are two types of project risks, namely, negative risks and positive risks. A negative risk is also called a threat. This type of risk has the potential to harm a project and its objectives. Positive risks are called opportunities. These can benefit a project's objectives.

One type of situation that presents obvious threats and opportunities in a project is when innovation has been introduced. Innovation implies that you're trying a new way of doing things instead of following an old, well established principle or procedure. However, you don't know how the innovation is going to work out. So with innovation comes an increase in project risk.

Let's use an example. You are managing a project to upgrade a gym so it features state of the art equipment and facilities. You've applied some innovative thinking to the technical regulatory and marketing areas of this project but you know there may be risks as a result.

[Technical] For technical innovation, you've decided to use a range of gym equipment that a new company has manufactured. You've researched the equipment and heard good reports so far, but this range hasn't been on the market for long. There is a possible threat that the equipment won't deliver on its promises. However, there is also a good opportunity. The gym is a forerunner in using what could become a popular and well respected brand of gym equipment.

[Regulatory] The current layout of the gym is outdated so you decide to completely redesign it. The new plans affect the regulatory area of this project because they must adhere strictly to new health and safety regulations. For example, the government has recently changed the rules about the number and location of fire escape routes.

You have to ensure that the new layout complies. The threat is that if the new layout does not pass these regulations, the gym could face fines and have to spend time and money on redesign. The opportunity is that the gym will be safe for members and management won't have to worry about health and safety regulations for years to come.

[Marketing] As a marketing strategy you've decided to install touch screens on the new cardio

Risk Management Professional (PMBOK 6)

vascular gym equipment which enables users to watch television, listen to music and program their workouts. The possible threat is that you could be excluding people who are not technologically minded from using the machines. The opportunity is that you'll attract members who enjoy using this type of technology.

All projects face risks of some kind. Being able to spot risks means being able to spot a possible, unexpected event that may have an impact on the project objectives. But you should also be able to determine whether the risk is good or bad.

Project risk management includes planning for risks and risk responses. It also means identifying, analyzing, and monitoring risks throughout your project to ensure they pose the least threat to your project as possible. All projects carry risk. So there's no avoiding it. Projects, no matter how small or simple, have some level of uncertainty and if you're using an Agile approach there is even more uncertainty due to the nature of the Agile methodology.

But there are some best practices you can consider to reduce risk for adaptive project environments.

First, you may want to introduce frequent reviews at incremental stages of the product development. This can help catch any issues before they cause more problems. You may also want to make use of cross-functional teams. This increases knowledge sharing and risk understanding.

And you should also approach requirements with the frame of mind that they are open to change. What this means is that requirements are updated regularly and can be re-prioritized based on the needs at any given time throughout the project life cycle. Making these considerations will help you greatly when trying to manage risk in Agile based projects.

1.2. Types of Project Risks

In this topic we're going to use our definition of project risk to examine more closely what it means that project objectives would be impacted by unforeseen events.

First of all, which part of a project do you think is the riskiest? The truth is, project risks can be found at any point throughout a project's life cycle. To help you identify potential risks, you should think of what events could cause risks and which areas of the project may be affected by each of those events.

These are just some of the areas that may be affected by risks. Project, budget and schedule, scope and project requirements, technical and hardware, project management processes, personnel, political, legal and contracts and business environment and management.

Over the next few minutes, you'll consider the various risks in three different projects. First, let's say you've been assigned a project to manage. But the project sponsor, who is the person who has to sign off on everything, is often out of the office. He's difficult to reach and often does not reply to messages. The absentee project sponsor could cause many uncertainties for the project. The culmination of these risks could lead to project failure.

[Schedule] If the project sponsor is not available to make decisions, the schedule may be affected. You may have to waste time trying to track him down and the project may fall behind schedule because decisions are not made quickly enough.

[Budget] If the project's sponsor is always absent, the budget may suffer because you may find it difficult to get additional funding you need to complete tasks.

[Team morale] Team members may feel a lack of commitment to the project on the part of the project sponsor and might be unsure about what is expected of them.

[Scope] The project may suffer from scope grade because of an absentee project sponsor. Uncontrolled changes and bad scope definition will contribute to this. It may also happen that he appears midway through the project and asks for significant changes if he hasn't been involved in the requirements identification process.

Now, take the example of a construction company that's bidding for a government contract to build a wind energy farm. The company has never worked for government before. So this will be a new experience for them. The company faces several negative risks in this project. The risk of the unknown in using new subcontractors which may cause schedule and supply problems.

The environmental risk, because of the many regulations you must now comply with. And the political risk, because the location of the wind energy farm has caused a public outcry. The local government might step in and change the requirements, leading to more time and expenses for approval.

However, this project also faces some opportunities. The risk of accepting the project could result in the company being contracted to develop full-scale wind energy farms if this test project is successful.

Finally, take the example of a clothing company that wants to upgrade its IT system so it can strengthen its online presence. Let's identify some risks here. [Scope and project quality risks] The risk exists that the project could suffer from scope or quality issues. For example, if the quality control team doesn't thoroughly test the accuracy of the database, there may be ordering or billing problems once the systems go live.

The business risks include the possibility that the initial designs of the network or the online business won't be suitable for the business work. The technical risks include the problems that may occur when integrating the existing and upgraded systems, especially if the software hasn't been implemented in other projects.

In summary, part of managing a project is being able to identify risk. It helps to remember that a risk can be positive or negative, and that it can impact any part of a project. You can find risk in almost all areas of a project, some areas include, the budget, schedule, the project plan, project scope, and project requirements. You may also face technical, hardware, personnel, political, legal, contractual, environmental and business issues.

1.3. Reducing the Uncertainty of Risk

For risk management to succeed, you must respond proactively to risks. If you only respond once an event occurs, you will waste time and resources needlessly trying to manage it. It's a lot better to avoid fires than to waste time and resources putting them out.

Risk management has two central roles. Reducing uncertainty about identified risks and determining appropriate responses for possible risks that can't be avoided. These roles enable you to eliminate some of the negative outcomes and take advantage of positive outcomes if a risk event occurs. In this topic, we're going to talk about the first aspect, reducing uncertainty.

To reduce uncertainty in a project, you determine the probability of a risk occurring, the consequences and impact, and the potential causes. Probability is the chance of something happening.

It can be low, high, or anything in-between. For example, you determine how likely it is that heavy rain will stop construction work on your project during the summer. Based on your experience, you feel that this risk is low. You consult historical records and discover that there's actually an 8% chance of heavy summer rainfall for that region.

Now let's talk about impact. Remember, a risk can impact any area of a project, cost, schedule, quality or scope. When you consider the impact of a risk, you look at its severity. Risks are often rated as low, medium, or high, based on the impact they would have on meeting the project's objectives.

It is useful to quantify the ratings and give each a threshold. For example, a risk may be low if it would impact the budget by less than 10% [medium if the impact is between 10 to 20%] and high if the impact is greater than 20%.

Quantifying ratings is helpful to standardize the language that the project team uses to describe risk impact. The severity of the impact of a risk often depends on the stage the project is at when the risk event occurs. A risk's impact might even increase as the project continues.

Early on in the project, before you've spent the budget and used up the schedule, the impact of a risk, such as quality issues or a change in scope, would be relatively low. But when you are approaching the end of a project and there is not much room left in the budget or schedule to absorb change, the impact of the risk is much greater.

The third aspect of reducing uncertainty is to determine potential causes. If you identify the causes for a specific risk, you can find ways to

Risk Management Professional (PMBOK 6)

avoid or mitigate it. To mitigate means to reduce its probability, impact, or both. You can also explore reasons why a risk is likely to happen and why it will have the impact you predict.

For instance, you identify the risk of losing a senior member of the project team. The likelihood of this happening depends on many factors. Including her current job satisfaction, her salary, and whether she's already being recruited by another company. The impact to your project of losing her depends partly on the scope of the project for which she is responsible. It also depends on how difficult it will be to find and train her replacement.

Next, you consider the cause of the risk. The developer is satisfied with her current position, but she said she'll change jobs for a better salary. You can't afford to lose her skills during this project so you find a practical response to the risk. To encourage her to stay for the duration of the project, you offer a retention bonus that is tied to the completion of the project.

The more you can control the cause of a risk, the better you can mitigate it. With the senior developer, you mitigated the risk by controlling its cause. But sometimes you have little or no control over the cause. For instance, a project may depend heavily on oil. You have no control over the price of oil and a rapid price increase could impact the project severely.

In summary, risk management is about reducing uncertainty about identified risks, and determining appropriate responses to risk. To assess a risk, you determine its probability, investigate its consequences and impacts, and establish its causes.

1.4. Understanding Risk Responses

Risk management has two central roles, reducing uncertainty about identified risks, and determining appropriate responses for when risk events do occur. In this topic, we're going to talk about the second aspect, determining responses.

Developing appropriate responses to identified risks during the planning stage is the most important way to manage and control risk in a project. If the risk that you've identified doesn't occur, great.

But if it does occur and you're prepared for it, then you implement the response. You then follow up by asking how effective your planned response was at controlling the damage caused by the risk. Or if the risk was positive and posed an opportunity, was the response effective at maximizing the benefits to the project?

Here are some appropriate risk responses. Increasing the budgets so that it includes a contingency reserve. Adjusting the schedule according to the new conditions after the risk event.

Stacking resources, which means moving staff within the project to handle bottlenecks or the situation more effectively. Changing the scope when this is beneficial or unavoidable. For example, say the funding is cut. You would scale back the work to make sure you still come in on budget, or closing the project prematurely in the case of a catastrophic event.

Here is an example of how adding a contingency to your budget can help you manage schedule risk. In order to win a contract, a construction project sets an aggressive schedule.

The schedule risk is high, because any delays at all will cause schedule overruns, which will put project success at stake. You decide to add a contingency reserve of 20% to the budget in case you need to hire extra staff to complete the work on time.

There are two categories that all risks fall into. Known unknowns, which are risks that you can predict and therefore mitigate against. Known unknowns are risks that you can identify early on the project based on events that have occurred in similar past projects, or they can simply be common sense predictions about what might possibly go wrong.

One common source of known unknowns is budget overruns. You can often predict these based on increases your expecting and resource, and production cost. Another common known unknown is the risk of a customer changing the scope late in the project, which means you have to redesign the

Risk Management Professional (PMBOK 6) products features.

Then there are unknown unknowns, which are unforeseen events that no one identified as possible risks before they happened. A fire that destroys a production facility and a natural disaster such as an earthquake are unknown unknowns that you can't predict.

Other kinds of risks that are difficult to predict to include communication breakdowns, power failures, and loss of data from a virus on your network that your security measures couldn't detect.

So in summary, even when you can't avoid a risk, you can develop an appropriate response, such as adjusting the schedule, increasing the budget, or moving staff on the project. Risk management is also about maximizing the benefits from positive risks. Risks can be either known unknowns or unknown unknowns.

1.5. Inputs to Plan Risk Management

Plan risk management is the process of defining how to conduct risk management activities for a project. By planning carefully, you increase the chances of success for managing risk in your project.

Planning risk management is important because it ensures that you set aside enough resources and time for risk management activities. It also enables you and the project stakeholders to establish an agreed upon basis for evaluating project risks.

There are five inputs to the plan risk management process. The first is the project management plan. To identify and plan for how to manage risks, you need to consider all the approved subsidiary plans and make sure the risk management plan aligns with them.

The cost management plan contains information that may impact risk management planning such as cost control thresholds, procedures to account for currency exchange rate fluctuations and the rationale for strategic funding choices.

The schedule management plan contains the schedule control thresholds and control accounts that are to be used for measuring scheduled performance. In general, the communications

Risk Management Professional (PMBOK 6)

management plan defines the interactions that will occur on the project. The communications management plan will allow the risk planning team to identify who will be available to share information about risk and when.

The next input is the project charter. It contains the description of the project's deliverables and objectives. Understanding the project deliverables and their complexity, helps the team determine the complexity of the whole risk management effort.

With regards to project constraints, everything that limits the team's options is usually listed. This might include a predefined budget or a critical schedule milestone issued by the customer. Constraints often represent areas of risk because the impact is high if they need to be changed for any reason. For example, any project with an imposed completion date.

Risks originate from any aspect of the project that may cause delays and jeopardize the finish date.

Project assumptions should also be identified as risks. You can express each risk in terms of the potential that the assumption proves to be false. For example, the scoped features and functionality of a new software program are based on the assumption that users will be running a specific version of a compatible software. The risk associated with this assumption is that users maybe running an older version.

Another input would include relevant project documents. For planning risk management, the stakeholder register is used. [A stakeholder register displays.] It provides information about the project stakeholders including their contact information, the role they will play, their requirements and expectations. And classification based on the stakeholders potential influence over project outcomes.

And two other inputs to the plan risk management process are enterprise environmental factors and organizational process assets. One of the key enterprise environmental factors to consider is the risk tolerance level of the organization and its stakeholders.

There may also be risk thresholds set by the organization. The last input, organizational process assets are your organization's existing risk management policies and guidelines.

These six organizational process assets can influence the plan risk management process. Risk categories that are typical for the types of projects your company carries out. Templates that may be used to develop the risk management plan, risk register, or other documents used for risk planning.

Risk Management Professional (PMBOK 6)

Risk statement formats that are typically used for risk planning in your organization. Roles and responsibilities of the individuals within your company who oversee risk planning, authority levels for decision making, and finally lessons learned from risk management activities in previous similar projects.

1.6. Tools and Techniques to Plan Risk Management

Imagine trying to manage a project where you aren't sure what the project's potential risks are. In order to effectively monitor and control the risks on a project, it is important to first plan for potential risks.

To do so, you use specific tools and techniques. One vitally important technique is data analysis. You use data analysis methods, such as a stakeholder analysis, to perform a preliminary and high level assessment of the project's risk management context.

Risk management context has two components. One is stakeholder risk attitude. How much tolerance do your stakeholders have for risk? Is their overall risk appetite high or low? A technique you could use to assess this is a stakeholder risk profile analysis. The other component of risk management context is the project's overall risk exposure.

One tool for assessing risk exposure is a strategic risk scoring sheet. [A strategic risk scoring sheet displays. It has various rows and columns. The column headers are Rating Factor, Weight, Score, and Assigned Score.] It lists typical areas of risk exposure, such as financial, technical and

Risk Management Professional (PMBOK 6)
environmental, and has spaces for you to score your project on each point.

Expert judgment, another technique, takes input from experts from all the different project areas. Drawing on perspectives and experience of many people. Several types of people could offer risk management advice.

Project team members, external stakeholders, functional managers or other project managers who have worked on projects in the same area, and subject matter experts who have risk management experience.

Meetings is the final tool and technique of the plan risk management process. As a project manager, it's typically your responsibility to facilitate these meetings and guide your team in making timely and appropriate decisions.

You need to be careful not to overlook individuals who have a legitimate interest in your project. You could encounter delays or cost overruns at a later stage if such individuals decide to make their ideas known after a project's developments have begun.

Also, you shouldn't try to do everything in one big meeting that may get out of hand and achieve little. You need to arrange your stakeholders into logical groups that have specific aims. You then set

Sorin Dumitrascu

up a series of smaller meetings with each group.

1.7. The Risk Management Plan

The first one we'll talk about is methodology. Methodology is a description of how you plan to execute the risk management plan. You need to include the methods your team will use during risk identification and analysis. The tools you'll use and where to find sources of risk information.

Methods for identifying risks include brainstorming sessions, interviewing subject matter experts, and assumptions analysis. You can also identify causes of risks with process flow diagrams and explore causes and impacts by using cause and effect diagrams. Methods for analyzing risks include probability and impact assessments using a probability and impact matrix, probability distributions, and simulations.

Strategies for responding to risks range from avoiding and transferring risks to mitigating and accepting the risks. The strategies the team chooses depends on the nature of the risk and the risk tolerance of the performing organization and stakeholders.

Methods for monitoring and controlling risks include status meetings to assess project performance and reassess risk. The methods and tools you use depend on the complexity and nature of the project. They also depend on the budget and time that has been approved for risk management activities. The more complex the project is and the more budget you have to work with, the more tools you will be able to use to manage risk.

The roles and responsibilities section should identify the lead, support and risk management team members for each type of activity in the risk management plan. It should also include each of their responsibilities in managing risk. [Budgeting] The funding section of the risk management plan contains information on the estimated resources, funds and contingencies that will be required for risk management activities.

The timing section of the risk management plan typically includes when and how often risk management activities will take place. It also includes the activities that are associated with risk management in a project schedule. Bear in mind that adding the risk activities to the project schedule may push the final product delivery date out too far. If that happens, you may need to make compromises so that the schedule remains viable.

The first one we'll talk about is methodology. Methodology is a description of how you plan to execute the risk management plan. You need to include the methods your team will use during risk

Risk Management Professional (PMBOK 6) identification and analysis. The tools you'll use and where to find sources of risk information.

Methods for identifying risks include brainstorming sessions, interviewing subject matter experts, and assumptions analysis. You can also identify causes of risks with process flow diagrams and explore causes and impacts by using cause and effect diagrams. Methods for analyzing risks include probability and impact assessments using a probability and impact matrix, probability distributions, and simulations.

Strategies for responding to risks range from avoiding and transferring risks to mitigating and accepting the risks. The strategies the team chooses depends on the nature of the risk and the risk tolerance of the performing organization and stakeholders.

Methods for monitoring and controlling risks include status meetings to assess project performance and reassess risk. The methods and tools you use depend on the complexity and nature of the project. They also depend on the budget and time that has been approved for risk management activities. The more complex the project is and the more budget you have to work with, the more tools you will be able to use to manage risk.

The roles and responsibilities section should

identify the lead, support and risk management team members for each type of activity in the risk management plan. It should also include each of their responsibilities in managing risk. [Budgeting] The funding section of the risk management plan contains information on the estimated resources, funds and contingencies that will be required for risk management activities.

The timing section of the risk management plan typically includes when and how often risk management activities will take place. It also includes the activities that are associated with risk management in a project schedule. Bear in mind that adding the risk activities to the project schedule may push the final product delivery date out too far. If that happens, you may need to make compromises so that the schedule remains viable.

1.8. Sample Risk Management Plan

The risk management plan contains the overall plan for managing risk throughout the project's life cycle, broken down into different sections. In this topic, we're going to walk through a simple risk management plan.

Tina is a project manager for a large urban hospital. She is organizing a project to automate the hospital's accounts receivable system. Tina estimates the project will take 18 months and require a team of 15 full-time dedicated programmers. Risk management planning will be extremely important because stakeholders have a very low risk tolerance.

With regards to methodology, she'll facilitate meetings with the project team and key stakeholders to make decisions about how to conduct the risk management process. She'll also speak with each of the stakeholders right away to find out if there have been any changes in their levels of risk tolerance.

She's also planning a series of meetings to define the risk management approach. Once she and her team have identified and categorized the risks, they'll meet weekly throughout the project's life cycle to discuss how they're dealing with risks and if they can improve on their processes.

In terms of roles and responsibilities, the hospital has its own risk management department, so Tina will invite key personnel to her weekly risk management meetings. For this project specifically, risk tolerance is almost nonexistent, so the funding for risk management activities will be extensive. Tina estimates risk management costs will run around $5,000.

In terms of timing, she will add the planned risk management activities to the project schedule. She has estimated the risk identification and analysis activities will take one week, plus one day per week throughout the remainder of the project. The hospital has a predefined approach to risk categories and definitions. She will use the required templates and talk with other project managers to learn about their experience with the hospital's risk management processes.

For reporting formats, Tina expects to use Excel spreadsheets to record risk information and to use for tracking purposes. Since Excel data can be easily exported as charts, she will use that tool for any presentations to stakeholders, and in the weekly reports that get emailed to everyone.

Finally, since the budget is so tight, there will be fairly low thresholds on the impact readings. Anything over 3% above estimated cost and

Risk Management Professional (PMBOK 6)
duration is going to have high impact. For probability, a moderate probability will be 50%, and anything over 75% is high. This is a very simplistic example, but hopefully it was useful in allowing you to understand the thought process behind putting a risk management plan together.

1.9. The Risk Probability and Impact Matrix

An important part of the risk management plan is a section that defines how probability and impact will be defined for your particular project. This topic explains how to develop those definitions and create a probability and impact matrix. There is a distinct difference between risk probability and risk impact.

Risk probability is the likelihood that an event will occur. Flipping a coin is the classic example of explaining this concept. When you flip a coin, there's always 0.5 probability, or a 50% chance of getting heads, and an equal probability of getting tails.

Probability is sometimes expressed as a number from 0 to 1. 0 indicates there is no probability of the event or risk occurring, whereas 1 indicates a 100% certainty that the event or risk will occur. The probability that an event will occur, plus the probability that it won't, always = 1.

Risk impact is the amount of danger, or opportunity, the risk event poses to the project. It is concerned with the effect the risk event will have on the projects objective, such as meeting the budget, finishing on schedule, and satisfying customers' expectations.

Risk Management Professional (PMBOK 6)

There are two types of scales you can use to rate probability and impact, a cardinal scale, or an ordinal scale. A cardinal scale measures probability and impact from 0 or very low, to 1, which is very high. An ordinal scale ranges from low to high. The project team must decide which scale is most appropriate to express risk probability and impact.

Here are examples of cardinal and ordinal equivalence when combined to express risk probability.

Very unlikely equals 0, somewhat unlikely could be 0.3, may happen could be 0.5, likely 0.7, very likely 0.9, and certain to happen 1.0.

Risk impact can also be expressed as cardinal or ordinal values. These are the equivalent values expressed in a typical high-high to low-low scale. Low-low = 0.05. Low equals = 0.25. Medium = 0.5. High = 0.75. And high- high = 1.

In order to rate the impact of any given risk, [A table depicting Example of Definitions for Probability and Impacts displays. It has various rows and columns.

The column headers are Scale, Probability, and Impact on Project Objectives. Impact on Project Objectives is further divided into Time, Cost, and you must understand what criteria will be used to determine a low, medium, and high rating. This is something the project manager and team will determine together. For example, if a risk event causes the budget to go over by 10%, will you consider the impact low or moderate?

And what is the threshold between moderate and high impact? The answers to this questions form the definitions of impacts for your project. You can develop a table that reflects how impact is defined for each objective. You can list the scale down the left column and the impact on project objectives across the top of the row. The definitions appear in the intersecting cells, for example, if you know that a risk will create a cost of over a million dollars, it will be assigned a score of high, depending on the type of scale you're using.

A probability and impact matrix allows you to look up a combined risk rating for any given risk.

For example, if you knew the risk of exceeding the budget has a 0.5 probability and a point 0.8 impact, you would multiply these two numbers together to arrive at a combined risk rating of 0.4.

The probability and impact matrix is good to use if you're using a cardinal number scale. But what if you're using an ordinal scale with low medium and high as the ratings?

In that case, you need a probability and impact matrix that translates you're two ordinal values into

Risk Management Professional (PMBOK 6)

a combined probability and impact rating. In other words in each probability and impact combination has a risk rating.

As this matrix indicates when medium probability is paired with low impact, the risk rating is low. When medium probability is paired with high impact, the risk rating is high. Whichever type of scale you use for your project, ordinal or cardinal, the probability, and impact matrix, and your impact definition table, should be included in the risk management plan.

1.10. Exercise: Planning Risk Management

In this exercise, you'll demonstrate your ability to effectively manage potential risks by planning ahead and assessing their impact, probability, and cause.

In this exercise, you'll demonstrate that you can
1. define risk and recognize examples
2. recognize how to reduce uncertainty
3. recognize examples of common risk responses
4. identify the inputs, tools and techniques, and output of the Plan Risk Management process, and
5. rate risks using a probability and impact matrix

Question

How is project risk defined?

Options:

1. An event that could possibly happen and that would impact one or more project objectives

2. An old, well-established principle or procedure

3. A delay which has caused a revision in the project schedule

4. An upcoming status review for meeting

Risk Management Professional (PMBOK 6)
project objectives

Answer

Option 1: This is the correct option. A risk means being able to spot a possible, unexpected event that may have an impact on the project objectives.

Option 2: This is an incorrect option. A risk is a future unexpected event that may have an impact on the project objectives.

Option 3: This is an incorrect option. The delay has already occurred. It is not an uncertain future event that will have an impact on the project objectives, which is what risk is.

Option 4: This is an incorrect option. Risk refers to an unexpected event that may have an impact on the project objectives. It is unrelated to upcoming status reviews for meeting project objectives.

Question

You are the project manager for a project to develop a new range of designer kitchen appliances for a large electronics company.

What are the three examples of risks that the project could encounter?

Options:

1. A bout of flu has hit some team members and may affect more, which could result in the project

being understaffed

2. The cleaning staff for the offices of the performing organization are threatening a slowdown in their work until certain trade union demands are met

3. Scope creep could occur because some of the initial designs for the appliances weren't properly approved

4. One of the prototype appliances has a technical malfunction that may also be present in other appliances in the range

5. A fire damaged the studio where the appliance designers were working, so the project schedule had to be adjusted to allow for the move into a newly equipped studio

Answer

Option 1: This is a correct option. The likelihood of the other team members catching the flu is uncertain, but it could happen. If it does happen, it will impact the project's personnel requirements.

Option 2: This is an incorrect option. This is a risk for the company but not a direct risk to the project. Even if cleaning services are slow, the design project would likely be able to progress.

Option 3: This is a correct option. There is an uncertain possibility that scope creep could occur because of incorrect designs being used. If scope creep does occur, this will impact the project's scope objectives.

Option 4: This is a correct option. The discovery of the technical problem causes an uncertainty that the other appliances will have the same problem. This may impact the project's technical objectives.

Option 5: This is an incorrect option. Although the fire and the move to the new studio may have impacted the project, these events have already occurred. It is not an uncertain future event.

Question

What three factors of risk do you need to determine in order to reduce uncertainty?

Options:

1. The likelihood of the risk happening
2. The impact of the risk
3. The cause of the risk
4. The chances that the majority of stakeholders are aware of the risk
5. The most recent reference to the risk in the news

Answer

Option 1: This is a correct option. To reduce uncertainty in a project, you determine the likelihood of a risk occurring. This is the probability of something happening, which can be low, high, or anything in between.

Option 2: This is a correct option. To reduce uncertainty in a project, you determine the consequences and impact of the risk. Risks are often rated as low, medium, or high based on the impact they would have on meeting the project's objectives.

Option 3: This is a correct option. To reduce uncertainty in a project, you determine the potential causes of the risk. If you identify the causes of a specific risk, you can find ways to avoid or mitigate it.

Option 4: This is an incorrect option. To reduce uncertainty in a project, you determine the likelihood of a risk occurring, the consequences and impact, and the potential causes. Whether stakeholders are aware of the risk has no bearing on any of these.

Option 5: This is an incorrect option. To reduce uncertainty in a project, you determine the likelihood of a risk occurring, the consequences and impact, and the potential causes. Whether the risk was covered in the media has no bearing on any of these.

Question

What are the four examples of common risk responses?

Options:

Risk Management Professional (PMBOK 6)
1. Increase the project budget
2. Adjust the project schedule
3. Stack project resources
4. Change the project scope
5. Outsource the project to another company
6. Ignore the risk until it's more likely

Answer

Option 1: This is a correct option. A common response to risk is to allocate more toward the budget to handle the risk. This could reduce the negative impact of the risk on the project.

Option 2: This is a correct option. If the risk becomes a reality, it is common to change the project schedule to get the project completed when and as necessary to mitigate the risk.

Option 3: This is a correct option. It is common to stack resources by, for example, moving staff members onto a project to adjust the project completion and mitigate the risk.

Option 4: This is a correct option. Reducing the scope is a common response to a risk. The project can be completed successfully but with a reduced scope.

Option 5: This is an incorrect option. Outsourcing the project is not a common response to handling risks and may exacerbate the problem.

Option 6: This is an incorrect option. Ignoring

risks is not a common response. It leads to inadequate preparation that could impact the project negatively.

Question

The Plan Risk Management process has specific inputs.

Match the inputs with the information they provide.

Options:

A. Project charter
B. Communications management plan
C. Stakeholder register

Targets:

1. Helps to answer questions about the product and how much overall uncertainty the project team will face as the project is planned and carried out
2. Defines the interactions that will happen during the project
3. Indicates key players in the project and what their expectations are

Answer

Because the project charter contains a description of the deliverables and objectives, it is an important place to look when identifying the extent of risk in a project. It also provides clues for potential project risks such as whether your project

Risk Management Professional (PMBOK 6) has an imposed completion date.

The communication management plan outlines who will be available to share information about risks and when. It is one of the components of the project management plan, which – in addition to providing communications guidelines – establishes the activities and criteria for planning, structuring, and controlling the project costs and schedule.

Because influential stakeholders can impact project success, the stakeholder register is an important input to risk management planning.

Question

Match the Plan Risk Management process inputs with the information they provide. Each process may match to more than one type of information.

Options:

A. Enterprise environmental factors
B. Organizational process assets

Targets:

1. Risk tolerance levels
2. Policies and guidelines that already exist in the organization
3. Risk attitudes of stakeholders within your organization
4. Authority levels for decision making that can influence risk management activities

Answer

Risk tolerance levels are an enterprise environmental factor that demonstrate the organization's willingness to embrace high-threat situations or unwillingness to forego high-opportunity conditions.

Policies and guidelines that already exist in the organization are organizational process assets that are used to plan risks

Risk attitudes are an enterprise environmental factor that demonstrate the organization's willingness to embrace high-threat situations or unwillingness to forego high-opportunity conditions

Authority levels for decision making that can influence the process are organizational process assets used to plan risks

Question

What are the three tools and techniques used for the Plan Risk Management process?

Options:

1. Meetings
2. Risk reassessment
3. Risk audits
4. Variance and trend analysis
5. Expert judgment
6. Data analysis

Risk Management Professional (PMBOK 6)

Answer

Option 1: This is a correct option. Project teams hold planning meetings to develop the risk management plan. The project manager, selected team members, and stakeholders attend these meetings.

Option 2: This is an incorrect option. Project risk reassessment occurs during the Monitor Risks process, not within any of the planning processes.

Option 3: This is an incorrect option. Risk audits examine and document the effectiveness of risk responses in dealing with identified risks and their root causes. Risk audits occur during the Monitor Risks process.

Option 4: This is an incorrect option. Trends in the project's execution such as earned value management, should be reviewed using performance information. Variance and trend analysis occurs during the Control Risks process.

Option 5: This is a correct option. When planning risk management, consider the judgment and expertise of other groups or individuals with specialized training in – or knowledge of – the project's subject area.

Option 6: This is a correct option. Data analysis is used to understand and define the overall risk management context of the project, which includes stakeholder risk attitudes and overall risk exposure of the project.

Question

If you wanted to create a risk management plan, what sections should be included?

Options:

1. Methodology
2. Roles and responsibilities
3. Funding and timing
4. Risk categories
5. Schedule constraints
6. Quality baseline limits

Answer

Option 1: This is a correct option. You should include a methodology section, which is a description of how you'll perform risk management. Methodology also includes elements such as methods, tools, and where you might find risk data that you can use in the later processes.

Option 2: This is a correct option. You need to outline the roles and responsibilities of the people who are responsible for managing the identified risks and their responses for each type of activity.

Option 3: This is a correct option. In the funding section, you include assigned resources and estimated costs of risk management and its methods.

Risk Management Professional (PMBOK 6)

The information on when and how risk management processes will be performed is also included in the risk management plan.

Option 4: This is a correct option. An important part of risk planning is establishing risk categories. They are a way to systematically identify risks and provide a foundation for understanding them.

Option 5: This is an incorrect option. Schedule constraints could be one of many sources of information to consider when developing high-level categories of consideration for the risk management plan. It's most likely that schedule constraints would form part of the larger grouping of methodology or risk categories of consideration within the risk management plan.

Option 6: This is an incorrect option. The quality baseline is also a subsidiary of the project management plan. It doesn't form part of the risk management plan.

Question

Match each section of the project's risk management plan with its example.

Options:
A. Methodology
B. Roles and responsibilities
C. Funding

D. Timing

E. Reporting formats

Targets:

1. The project team identifies risks using brainstorming

2. Sue is responsible for controlling the risk of lost electronic data

3. An amount of $4,000 has been set aside to cover risk management activities

4. An extra month has been allotted to the project's schedule in case letters get lost in the mail

5. A graphic user interface (GUI) database will present the risk register

Answer

Brainstorming is a method of identifying risks. This information is contained in the methodology section of the risk management plan. Other possible methods are interviewing subject matter experts and identifying causes of risks with process flow diagrams.

The roles and responsibilities section of the risk management plan describes the people who are responsible for managing the identified risks for each type of risk management activity.

The project manager will always assign resources and estimate costs of all project risks. This is recorded in the funding section of the risk

Risk Management Professional (PMBOK 6) management plan.

When and how each risk management process should take place is recorded in the timing section of the risk management plan.

The risk register will take on the reporting format of a GUI database. The database will be used to maintain, update, analyze, and report to project participants.

Question

Match each section of a project's risk management plan with its example.

Options:

A. Tracking
B. Risk categories
C. Probability and impact
D. Revised stakeholder tolerances

Targets:

1. A system alert feature monitors and warns you about imminent threats to the project
2. The project risks are classified as technical, external, organizational, or project management
3. If a risk will cause an increase over 15%, it will get a rating of "high"
4. The customer's risk appetite has gone from moderate to virtually nonexistent

Answer

Sorin Dumitrascu

The alert feature is a tracking element described in the risk management plan for this project. It helps document the risk management activities and audit the risk management processes.

Risk categories help you systematically identify risks. Listing these specific categories in the risk management plan helps you align the risk categories with sections of the work breakdown structure.

This is an example of how impact may be defined for the project. Probability ratings would also have a range of low, moderate, and high and be expressed in terms of how likely risks are to occur.

The risk management plan may include stakeholders' risk tolerances and any changes in tolerance levels that have occurred since stakeholder analysis was performed.

Question

each overall risk rating to the corresponding probability and impact assessment. Ratings may match to more than one assessment.

Options:

A. Low
B. Medium
C. High

Targets:

1. A risk of inadequate training to carry out

Risk Management Professional (PMBOK 6)
project tasks has low probability and high impact

2. A risk of technology used for a project not being fit for purpose has low probability and medium impact

3. A risk of vendors supplying poor quality materials has medium probability and high impact

4. A risk of a delay in project funding approval has high probability and medium impact

Answer

A risk with low probability and high impact can be categorized as having a medium risk rating A risk with medium probability and low impact has a low risk rating

The assessed risk has a medium/high probability/impact rating, which means it should be placed in the high risk category

A risk with a high/medium probability/impact rating translates to an overall high risk rating

Question

How do you rate a risk with a probability and impact rating of 0.03?

The blue area of the probability and impact matrix is high risk, the light green is medium risk, and the dark green is low risk.

This probability and impact matrix contains numbers in the blue area, which are 0.36, 0.72, 0.28,

0.56, 0.4, and 0.24. The numbers in the light green area are 0.09; 0.14; 0.1; 0.12; 0.18; and 0.08. The numbers in the dark green area are 0.05; 0.04; 0.02; 0.03; 0.01; 0.06; and 0.07.

Options:

1. Low
2. Medium
3. High

Answer

Option 1: This is the correct option. The risk has a low rating because it falls within the low risk area of the probability and impact matrix.

Option 2: This is an incorrect option. This is not a medium risk. Rather, it has a low risk rating because it falls within the dark green, low risk area of the probability and impact matrix.

Option 3: This is an incorrect option. This is not a high risk. The risk actually has a low risk rating because it falls within the dark green, low risk area of the probability and impact matrix.

2. Identifying Risk (by PMBOK® Guide Sixth Edition)

2.1. Inputs to Identify Risks
2.2. Document Analysis
2.3. Brainstorming to Gather Data
2.4. Using Interviewing to Identify Risks
2.5. Using Root Cause Analysis to Identify Risks
2.6. Using SWOT Analysis to Identify Risks
2.7. Using Assumption and Constraint Analysis
2.8. Using Checklists to Identify Risks
2.9. Outputs of Identify Risks
2.10. Exercise: Identifying Risks

2.1. Inputs to Identify Risks

Project managers use the identify risks process to identify threats and opportunities that may impact a project and to document their characteristics. This process is iterative. It can occur many times during a project's life cycle, as new information about risks becomes available.

There are six different inputs to the identify risks process. First, there's the project management plan and relevant subsidiary plans contained within it. Risk management is a critical aspect of project management. So it should come as no surprise that you'll use a lot of the information in the project management plan to help you identify risks.

You'll use information in the Requirements Management Plan, Schedule Management Plan, Cost Management Plan, Quality Management Plan, Resource Management Plan, and the Risk Management Plan.

These plans contain information about potential cost overruns. Delays, quality defects, and how the project will be staffed. For example, you'll use the information in the risk management plan to assess team members' roles and responsibilities, the budget and schedule for risk management activities.

And categories of risk, such as external,

Risk Management Professional (PMBOK 6)

financial, operational and reputational risks. You'll also use the scope baseline, schedule baseline, and cost baseline. For example, the work breakdown structure, which is part of the scope baseline, provides critical information. You can work through the WBS to help identify risks at each level, and to gain an understanding of how the work has been structured.

The second input is any relevant project documents. In the identify risks process, this includes the assumption log, cost and duration estimates, the issue log, the lessons-learned register, requirements documentation, resource requirements, and the stakeholder register. For example, the assumption log identifies assumptions about the project.

Assumptions always carry the risk of being false, so they may help identify risks. For instance, the assumption that demand for the software will be strong, together with the constraint of strong competition, should lead you to identify a serious risk. A competitor could launch a similar product before yours. They would then benefit from the strong market demand and possibly eliminate demand for your software.

Cost and duration estimates enable you to predict and quantify the risks of costs or schedule overruns or the opportunities for budget or schedule savings. Say, you're exploring the risk that an activity will cost more than planned. You begin by looking at a low optimistic cost estimate, and then compare this with a pessimistic estimate based on high resource costs. In the end, you determine there is a very high risk of a cost overrun for this activity and document it as a legitimate risk for the project.

And like the roles and responsibilities outlined in the risk management plan, the Stakeholder Register records the names and details of people you can consult to help identify and characterize risks.

Agreements are another input. If you're using externally procured resources, the agreements with your external vendors, most likely detail milestone dates, the type of contract you have, acceptance criteria, and specific rewards or a penalties for meeting or missing agreed upon terms.

This information provides key risk data. Like agreements, if you are purchasing materials or services from external vendors at any point during a project, procurement documents also contain information that can help you identify risks to your project.

There are two other inputs to the identify risks process, enterprise environmental factors and organizational process assets. Examples of

Risk Management Professional (PMBOK 6) enterprise environmental factors that can help you to identify risks include the following. Industry wide risks outlined in risk studies or academic papers. These can highlight particular threats or opportunities.

Industrial benchmarking. You can identify risk areas where you see that your project specifications or plans deviate from the industrial benchmarks and risk attitudes. For instance, highly risk averse stakeholders could be a benefit or a risk in themselves.

Organizational process assets include historical project data and lessons learned which can be rich sources of information about risks in previous projects. These can help you identify similar risks in a current project. For instance, a risk statement template developed during a past project might incorporate useful experiences that can help you identify risks in a current project.

2.2. Document Analysis

Identifying risks is critical to your project's success, and there are a lot of useful tools to help you do that. In fact, there are six tools and techniques for identifying risks. These include expert judgment, data gathering techniques which include brainstorming, checklists, and interviews.

Data analysis techniques including root cause analysis, assumption and constrain analysis, SWOT analysis, and document analysis. Interpersonal and team skills including facilitation, prompt lists, and meetings. In this topic, we're going to look at expert judgment, which is a technique you use in practically all project management processes, meetings, as well as one of the data analysis techniques, document analysis.

A very helpful method for identifying risks is using the expert judgment of anyone who has expertise or experience with managing risk on similar projects or products, or insight into the environment in which a project will be carried out.

Expert judgment comes from many project stakeholders, both internal and external, including yourself as the project manager. It can also include any other relevant experts. Some examples include subject matter experts, customer representatives, or

Risk Management Professional (PMBOK 6) project managers who have worked on similar projects.

Risk identification session should involve stakeholders with a diverse range of experience and expertise. Identifying risks often involves meetings in which project team members and other stakeholders analyze inputs with a focus on identifying risks based on the information available to them.

The main objective of the sessions is to identify risks and then categorize, clarify, and define them. The group should record as much information about risks as it can, which will help with further risk analysis and response planning later on.

A document analysis is a fancy term for a structured review of all of the relevant project documents that can help you identify risks. These documents include plans, assumptions, constraints, previous project files, contracts and agreements, and any technical documentation available. When conducting a document analysis, there are three activities that require special attention.

[Identify contradiction and gaps] It's important to identify any gaps and inputs or contradictions between them. For instance, if an industry report indicates that a key supplier for a project is bordering on bankruptcy, this will close a gap in the project information and identify a clear risk.

Another situation might involve a cost estimate being updated using recent prices, while a cost baseline uses older price estimates. In this case, updating the baseline to reflect the new estimates removes or reduces the risk that the activity will cost more than you budget for it.

Reviewers must check that the subsidiary management plans within the overall project management plan are complete, accurate, and realistic. Examples of problems you would look for are vague policy statements, unrealistic estimates, and information that claims to be factual, but is not backed up. These inaccuracies can pose serious risks for any project.

[Investigate constraints and assumptions] And you should also pay particular attention to the assumptions and constraints documented for the project. Identifying associated risks ensures they can be addressed early on. You also need to examine all assumptions concerning cost, duration, and quality that were used to derive the estimate's and project baselines. And document every risk associated with these assumptions.

As mentioned, the main goal of a document analysis is to categorize and define risks. A useful tool for doing that is the risk breakdown structure. It

Risk Management Professional (PMBOK 6) already contains general categories of risks, so it will guide experts in identifying and clarifying risks.

2.3. Brainstorming to Gather Data

There are six tools and techniques for identifying risks. They include expert judgment, data gathering techniques, which include brainstorming, checklists, and interviews. Data analysis techniques, including root cause analysis, assumption, and constraint analysis. SWOT analysis and document analysis, interpersonal and team skills including facilitation, prompt lists, and meetings. In this topic, we're going to focus on one of the useful data gathering techniques, brainstorming.

Brainstorming involves getting all the subject matter experts, team members, and other managers together, and prompting them to identify as many potential project risks as they can.

This is a good technique to use when experts and stakeholders are in close proximity and can easily meet in one place. It's good for generating ideas because one person's idea will often spawn others. It's also efficient and inexpensive. A single effective brainstorming session could conceivably identify most, if not all, project risks for a small to medium project in just a few hours.

Let's talk about some guidelines for running one of these brainstorming sessions. First of all, you should involve stakeholders who have diverse

Risk Management Professional (PMBOK 6)

backgrounds, viewpoints, and areas of expertise. Identifying risks isn't something the project manager or only a group of people with similar experience should do alone.

Input from a multi-disciplinary group is required to ensure that risks in particular areas aren't overlooked. For example, an internal project that involves developing a new product line should include members from the internal research and development, marketing, financial, operations, and project teams.

Next, do something to get peoples' brains warmed up. As the facilitator, you might allow a time of freestyle brainstorming about something totally different, like reasons why the original Star Wars movies were better than the latest ones. Or do some type of ice breaker to get people comfortable with others in the group.

Next, it's a good idea to structure the session somehow, maybe according to pre-identified categories like those found in the risk breakdown structure or in the work breakdown structure.

The secret of good brainstorming facilitation is to make sure everyone gets a chance to participate. You've probably heard this a thousand times, but make sure everyone understands the cardinal rule at the outset, no negative comments or criticizing anyone else's ideas. Also, no self-censorship that comes from a fear of sounding silly.

There are four basic rules to follow when brainstorming. First, you identify your objective or problem, then you record the ideas generated. The third rule is to make sure the session stays on track, and the final rule is to build on one another's ideas. Getting the session off on the right foot is important.

Here's what I would say to begin a session if I was facilitating one. We are here to identify, define, and categorize potential risks for our project. Our goal is to identify all likely risks for each of the categories. We will begin with the organization category. Just take turns stating the risks you think the project might face because of the organization.

I'll record them on the whiteboard. We'll spend five minutes or so on each category, then we'll start building on the ideas we have at that point. As a basic ground rule, no one is to criticize anyone else's ideas. At first, it's the quantity of ideas that's the important thing. We'll work on quality later. Okay, Jack, do you want to get us started?

Like I said, if it's a group of people who don't know each other, you could start with something easy and unrelated just to get the creative juices flowing. Make sure you bring someone along who can act as the scribe to record all the information

Risk Management Professional (PMBOK 6)

you put on the whiteboard, just so you don't lose any ideas. It's too difficult to facilitate the session and be the one responsible for preserving the ideas, or running the technology, if you're using a smartboard.

So that's brainstorming. It's a great data gathering method to use for anytime you need to quickly generate ideas about something. In this case, the risks your project faces. It's best used when you have a group of experts who can easily meet in the same geographic location.

2.4. Using Interviewing to Identify Risks

There are six tools and techniques for identifying risks. Expert judgment, data gathering techniques, which include brainstorming, checklists, and interviews.

Data analysis techniques including root cause analysis, assumption and constraint analysis, SWOT analysis, and document analysis. Interpersonal and team skills, including facilitation, prompt lists, and meetings. In this topic, we're going to look at interviewing, one of the useful methods for data gathering when identifying risks.

Interviewing is best used for subject matter experts or individuals who can't attend a group meeting for geographic reasons. It can also be used where it would be inappropriate to involve someone, like the project client or a user representative at another organization, in a brainstorming session with internal stakeholders. You then interview key stakeholders from the customer and supplier companies to elicit potential risks they foresee.

Go into the interview with the list of risks that were initially identified during a brainstorming or other type of idea generating session. To spark ideas in an interview, you can provide the person with the

Risk Management Professional (PMBOK 6)

project's work breakdown structure or a risk breakdown structure template along with risk assumptions. Once the interviewee has identified as many additional risks as is reasonable, you should revisit each risk in order to classify it.

Here are some types of questions that you might want to ask during an interview to identify potential risks. In general, can you think of any risk factors or areas of risk surrounding this project that we've overlooked?

Now that you've reviewed our initial list of identified risks, are there any you would add to the list?

Let's go through the list of risks and add a bit more detail so we can get a better sense of them, their causes, and their potential impacts. As you can tell, these questions let you drill down from general to more specific. Once you've identified potential risks, you need to ask clarifying questions to flesh out understanding and definitions of the risk. Then ask about the causes and impacts of these risks.

To categorize any new risks identified during the interview, you can group them based on risk source, area of the project affected, or project phase. Grouping risks based on their common root sources or causes is an effective strategy that can simplify the process of developing appropriate risk responses.

You can use the risk breakdown structure as the basis for doing this. You can choose to categorize risks based on the area of the project affected using the work breakdown structure. You can choose other useful categories, such as project phase, to determine areas of the project most exposed to risks.

Again, interviewing is useful when it is either impractical or inappropriate for stakeholders to brainstorm as a group. In some ways, it allows you to focus much better on getting the information you need when you have just one expert at a time.

2.5. Using Root Cause Analysis to Identify Risks

There are six tools and techniques you can use for the identify risks process. They include expert judgment, data gathering techniques, which include brainstorming, checklists, and interviews. Data analysis techniques, including root cause analysis, assumption and constraint analysis, SWOT analysis, and document analysis. Interpersonal and team skills including facilitation, prompt lists, and meetings. In this topic, we're going to focus on one of the data analysis methods, root cause analysis, and how you can use it to identify project risks.

Root cause analysis cannot only help you identify and manage potential risks, but also to develop preventive action. It involves investigating risks to identify their root causes. You can then address these causes instead of just the symptoms. Although a root cause analysis can be performed by an individual, it's best to gather a group of experienced experts for a brainstorming session. Varying perspectives and experience among stakeholders who understand the project, its product, and its environment can contribute to a better understanding of risks and their possible causes.

For each risk, the group involved in a root cause

analysis should ask the following examples of questions. What sequence of events may lead up to the risk event? What conditions would allow the event to occur? What other risks could also be caused by the central issue? Even after you've identified some of the possible causes of a risk, you should keep asking questions so that you can identify as many relevant causes as possible. Being thorough produces the best results.

In a root cause analysis, you usually find that risks have three basic types of potential causes. Physical causes relate to flaws in tangible items. There could be defects in the raw materials used in producing a product, or faults in the tools, machineries, or equipment used to produce the product.

Human causes of risks are the results of human error. Someone may either carry out an undesirable action or fail to carry out a desirable action. Human causes often lead to physical causes. For example, forgetting to recalibrate a machine may result in the machine causing physical defects in a product. Human causes may stem from various underlying factors, such as incompetence, absence, different understandings of what's required, or personality differences.

Organizational causes of risk relate to the

Risk Management Professional (PMBOK 6)

systems, processes, or policies that impact a project. These causes can be internal, as in the case of a faulty manufacturing process that neglects an important safety check. Or they may be external, such as bad weather, fussy customers, or a weakening national economy.

By identifying the risks and their underlying potential causes, you can explore which threats might result in a problem occurring. It's important to note that you can also use root cause analysis to find opportunities and explore which opportunities might result in a benefit to the project.

2.6. Using SWOT Analysis to Identify Risks

SWOT analysis is one of the data analysis methods used to identify risks and classify them into different types. SWOT stands for strengths, weaknesses, opportunities, and threats. Identifying risks within these categories gives you a broad view of the types of risks a project faces.

A project's strengths and weaknesses are internal factors that may influence the project team's ability to meet its objectives. The performing organization is often able to exert some control over a project's strengths and weaknesses. Opportunities and threats come from outside the performing organization. They are external factors that could help or harm a project.

To perform a SWOT analysis, you brainstorm with team members or a specially assigned risk identification team. A SWOT analysis can be fairly simple or complex and detailed. Generally, it's best to keep it as simple as possible, listing only factors that may have a definite impact on the project. It's important to remember that a SWOT analysis is usually highly subjective. So although it can provide good insights about the risks a project may face, it shouldn't be the only technique you use to identify risks.

Risk Management Professional (PMBOK 6)

The best way to set up a SWOT analysis is to create a simple grid with a square for each of the four factors [which are Strength, Weaknesses, Opportunities, and Threats.] . In the strengths section, you list the advantages or strong points that you and your organization have. Ask yourself if you and your team have any unique abilities, opportunities, or wisdom to offer the project.

In the weaknesses section, you list the things about you, your team, or your organization that are disadvantages. These are areas that could be improved upon or that may compromise the success of a project.

In the opportunities section, you list positive external factors that could benefit the project. For example, opportunities can arise from particular external events, new technology, changes in societal attitudes, or policy changes.

In the threats section, you list external factors that may disrupt, damage, or hinder the project in any way. Let's explore an example. Say you're managing a project to create an online shopping portal for a well- known department store. You and your team are ready to brainstorm all the possible risks that could affect the project, and you've drawn up a basic SWOT analysis grid.

In the strengths section, you identify your

organization's location as a strength. The client is situated nearby, so meetings and on-site work will be easy to arrange. The fact that your organization specializes in website design and has the required expertise is also a strength.

The weaknesses you identify are that the organization currently has poor cash flow and lacks resources due to its small size. These internal factors could affect your ability to deliver quality results on time. In the opportunities section, you note the potential for expansion in the field of website design [and online shopping] and for attracting more customers, especially if the project is successful. However, a threat the project faces is that ideas could easily be poached by bigger companies, which would decrease your competitiveness.

Once you and your team have brainstormed and filled in the sections of a SWOT analysis grid, you should refine it. To do this, you can apply the USED strategy. The letters in USED stand for four questions. How could we use each strength?

How could we stop each weakness? How could we exploit each opportunity? How could we defend against each threat? Answering these questions will help you identify potential responses to the identified risks. So that's SWOT analysis and how you use it to identify and define project risks.

2.7. Using Assumption and Constraint Analysis

Actor Alan Alda once said, begin challenging your own assumptions. Your assumptions are your windows on the world. Scrub them off every once in a while, or the light won't come in.

In project management, challenging the assumptions on which a project is based is an important aspect of identifying risks. Most actions are based on assumptions, which are often similar to educated guesses. For instance, in project management, you make assumptions about the availability of facilities, the skills of your workers and that equipment will work properly.

If you don't make assumptions in a project, it's likely you'll become bogged down with all the possible events and outcomes that could occur. So assumptions are necessary. By nature though, any assumptions has an associated risk, as it may prove to be untrue.

In project management, an assumption and constraint analysis is one of the data analysis methods you should use during the identify risks process. It involves identifying potential risks to a project by examining the validity of the assumptions on which it's based, as well as analyzing the constraints within. It also involves assessing the potential impact that false assumptions could have on the project.

During an assumption analysis, you address each identified assumption that you've made about your project with a question. If this assumption proves to be false, then what is the impact on the project? Assumption analysis should be an ongoing activity.

You'll continue having to make assumptions throughout a project and it's important that you record these and regularly review them to ensure they are valid. This helps ensure any associated risks are identified so that plans for protecting a project against them can be developed.

Generally, it's better if the individuals assessing assumptions are not the same individuals who originally identified the risks. That way they can remain as objective as possible. People often don't recognize their own assumptions.

During assumption analysis, we check for three things to assess whether an assumption is valid. [Inaccuracy] The first question you should ask is whether the assumption is based on accurate information. An assumption might prove to be false for various reasons.

Perhaps it was true at one stage but circumstances have changed. Perhaps it is only partially true, or perhaps it's completely false. The

Risk Management Professional (PMBOK 6)

important thing is to ensure that assumptions are soundly based on fact, especially when they form the basis for actions that will be taken in a project.

[Inconsistency] It's important to check that basic assumptions not only seem to be accurate, but are also consistent with the other facts available and known. You might not actually be able to spot a specific inaccuracy, but if several facts or assumptions don't seem to add up, it likely indicates a problem.

[Incompleteness] Even if a recorded assumption seems accurate and consistent with the other information you have, it may not tell you everything you need to know.

For example, it may prove valid only under specific circumstances or at particular times. When analyzing an assumption, it's important to obtain as much detail as you can about its basis and the circumstances surrounding it.

Constraints are limitations on your project, such as budget, schedule, or available resources. Simply accepting these constraints places restrictions on what you can accomplish. That is why analyzing your constraints is vital, as the situation could change.

If a resource that previously wasn't available suddenly becomes available, or if a previous deadline has been relaxed by your customer, this could open up opportunities for your project.

In order to analyze constraints, you follow the same steps as an assumption analysis. It is also an ongoing process. And you must determine that the constraint is valid. However, you ask the question a little differently. If this constraint could be removed or minimized, then how would it benefit the project?

Once a team has verified assumptions and constraints, identifying the associated risks involves determining how each assumption could impact the project if it proves false. False assumptions and constraints can have several negative impacts.

Budget overruns as a result of incurring expenses not originally anticipated. Unanticipated schedule delays. A lack of resources due to false assumptions about resource availability or the resources required to complete tasks. And a lack of supplies when they're needed due to false assumptions about how quickly the supplies could be obtained.

Once a team has identified the risks associated with project assumptions and constraints, it's in a position to plan for the impact of these potential risks. Bear in mind that it is not only the direct impact on the project you should be concerned with. A false assumption or constraint, particularly one

Risk Management Professional (PMBOK 6) that has a significant impact on the budget or schedule, can have indirect impacts.

For example, it might shake stakeholders' confidence and make them lose faith in the project management team. Or a serious issue can impact the level of morale of your team, thereby decreasing productivity or creativity. Analyzing assumptions and constraints carefully during the identify risks process can help prevent this from occurring.

2.8. Using Checklists to Identify Risks

There are six tools and techniques you can use for the identify risks process. Expert judgment, data gathering techniques which include brainstorming, checklists, and interviews.

Data analysis techniques including root cause analysis, assumption and constraint analysis, SWOT analysis, and document analysis. Interpersonal and team skills including facilitation, prompt lists, and meetings. In this topic, we're going to focus on one of the data gathering techniques you can use to identify risks. Checklists.

You are probably familiar with the concept of a checklist. This may be something as informal as a list of things you should remember to pack when going on holiday. Or it may be a list of the pre-flight checks the aircraft crew must make before your plane takes off. Checklist are an excellent way to identify the important issues that need to be considered and ensure that vital items are not overlooked.

In the context of the identify risks process, checklists are a tool you can use to create a list of project risks and assess whether the risks apply to the current project.

The entries in a risk checklist for a project are

Risk Management Professional (PMBOK 6) generally based on historical information from similar past projects such as old risk registers and lessons learned documentation.

You then assess whether those risks apply to the current project. Another source of risks for the checklist is the lowest level of the project's risk breakdown structure. It includes the potential risks that have already been identified for the project.

Reviewing risk registers from similar past projects is a good way to learn about potential risks that you should add to a risk checklist for your current project. Examining how a problem was dealt with in the past can be as important as identifying a risk in the first place. Also, it can give you greater insight into risks you have already identified.

The team for an electric car project, for instance, consults the risk register from an earlier project that involved manufacturing a hybrid vehicle. [A Risk Register displays. It has various rows and columns. The column headers are Tracking, RBS, WBS, Date, Description, Cause, Impact, Severity, Likelihood, and Risk response. It also lists the name of the project and the project manager.] The team notices that one of the major problems was that at the time of the vehicle's release, it wasn't compatible with the latest and most efficient battery. This meant that extra expenses had to be incurred to produce an adapter.

Consider the risk breakdown structure for a project to manufacture a range of electric cars. You can add each of the risks identified below the technical, external, organizational, and project management categories to a checklist. The team adds each potential risk to its risk checklist.

As a project unfolds, new information about potential risks will become available and the risk checklist should be updated and refined. Similarly, the risk checklist should be reviewed and updated during project closure to incorporate lessons learned during the project. It then becomes a useful resource for future projects.

In summary, using checklists for data gathering involves identifying project risks and compiling them into a list that can be assessed by members of the project team. The two main types of project documents that are typically used as a source of information for checklists are the risk breakdown structure and risk registers from similar previous projects.

2.9. Outputs of Identify Risks

The identify risks process results in three outputs, the risk register, risk report, and project documents updates. The risk register is a table that lists information about each of the risks you have identified during the process. It includes a description of each risk, its potential impact, and its root causes.

The risk register becomes an important input to all of the other project risk management processes. New and more detailed information continues to be added to the risk register as other risk management and general project management processes are carried out.

A risk register generally contains several columns of information. he first four columns in the example register [which are Tracking, RBS, WBS, and Date] enable you to track each risk and its context throughout the project lifecycle.

A tracking number uniquely identifies each recorded risk so that it can be easily referenced and monitored. The RBS column links each risk to its category within the risk breakdown structure. And the WBS column associates each risk with the work components it may affect within the work breakdown structure.

The Date column lists the date at which each risk was identified. Another identifying characteristic that could be included in the risk register is risk status, which could be recorded as pending, current, or ended. The Description column should contain a clear and concise description of each identified risk. The Cause column should identify the cause or causes of each identified risk. Identifying the root causes of risks is an important step in developing effective risk responses.

The Impact column should detail the potential impact of each identified risk on the project. This section of the register may be further divided to detail the impact of each risk on specific project objectives. The Severity and Likelihood columns indicate the extent to which each risk could impact the project and the probability of the risk occurring. The options for these measures could be classified, for example, as none, very low, low, medium, high, and very high.

The Risk Response column lists the responses planned for managing each of the identified risks. Responses may include accepting a risk if its cause lies outside of the management team's control, or adjusting the project plan to lessen its potential impact.

During the identify risks process, you may

Risk Management Professional (PMBOK 6)
develop several potential risk responses for each risk and determine several root causes for these risks. Information on causes and responses gathered during this process may be adjusted or further developed later.

For example, information gathered during the identify risks process feeds into the plan risk responses process. Where appropriate risk responses for all identified risks are fully defined.

The other two outputs of the identify risks process are the risk report and appropriate project documents updates. The risk report, like the risk register, is developed, revised, and updated as project work and other risk management processes are carried out.

It summarizes information about the overall project risks. For example, you may include the following types of information in a risk report. Your identified sources of project risk, including the most significant risk exposure drivers.

And a summary of the individual project risk information. Such as how many threats and opportunities are identified, how risks are distributed across the risk categories, and any specific risk metrics or trends you've identified while identifying risks.

And as a result of identifying risk, there are most

Sorin Dumitrascu

likely some project documents that need to be updated with any new relevant information you've discovered. For example, the assumption log, issue log, or lessons learned register may require updates as a result of identifying risks.

2.10. Exercise: Identifying Risks

Exercise Overview

In this exercise, you'll demonstrate your understanding of how to effectively manage risks to your project by first identifying what these risks are.

In this exercise, you'll demonstrate that you can
1. identify inputs to the Identify Risks process
2. recognize document analysis activities when identifying risks
3. describe how to use brainstorming and interviewing when identifying project risks recognize causes of project risks
4. identify the components of a SWOT analysis
5. identify questions to ask during an assumption and constraint analysis
6. identify sources of information for using checklists, and
7. recognize the outputs of the Identify Risks process

Question

What are some of the inputs to the Identify Risks process?

Options:

1. Risk management plan
2. Stakeholder register

3. Cost and duration estimates
4. Scope baseline
5. Cost management plan
6. Agreements
7. Activity list templates
8. Risk documentation format

Answer

Option 1: This is a correct option. The risk management plan identifies which team members are responsible for risk management in various areas, makes provisions for time and money required for risk management activities, and contains a risk breakdown to group risks based on their characteristics.

Option 2: This is a correct option. The stakeholder register records the names and details of people you can consult to help identify and characterize risks.

Option 3: This is a correct option. Cost and duration estimates enable you to predict and quantify the risks of cost or schedule overruns or the opportunities for budget or schedule savings.

Option 4: This is a correct option. The scope baseline, which includes the work breakdown structure and project scope statement, provides critical information.

Option 5: This is a correct option. The cost

Risk Management Professional (PMBOK 6)

management plan contains information about potential cost overruns, which will help you identify and characterize risks.

Option 6: This is a correct option. If you need externally-supplied resources, agreements will include important information related to milestone dates and acceptance criteria which may pose risks to the project.

Option 7: This is an incorrect option. Activity list templates simplify the process of recording and describing activities. However, you would use the descriptions of activities, rather than the templates, to help identify risks.

Option 8: This is an incorrect option. The format you use to document risks is important and must be consistent. However, it will not help you identify risks.

Question

What are some other inputs to the Identify Risks process?

Options:

1. Quality management plan
2. Resource management plan
3. Enterprise environmental factors (EEFs)
4. Organizational process assets (OPAs)
5. Procurement documents

6. Project documents
7. Risk management strategies
8. Total budget estimates

Answer

Option 1: This is a correct option. The quality management plan contains information about quality defects, an important indicator of risk.

Option 2: This is a correct option. The human resource management plan contains information about how the project will be staffed, which is an important indicator of risk.

Option 3: This is a correct option. Examples of EEFs that can help you identify risks include industry-wide risks outlined in risk studies or academic papers, industrial benchmarking, and risk attitudes.

Option 4: This is a correct option. OPAs include historical project data and lessons learned, which can be rich sources of information about risks in previous projects.

Option 5: This is a correct option. Examples of procurement documents include approved requests for proposals, contracts, statements of work, and agreements, which are important indicators of risk.

Option 6: This is a correct option. Project documents provide ongoing risk identification. They are mostly documents that become available as a

Risk Management Professional (PMBOK 6)

project progresses such as work performance reports and updated baselines.

Option 7: This is an incorrect option. This information becomes part of the risk management plan only once you've identified risks and formulated appropriate strategies for managing them.

Option 8: This is an incorrect option. Total budget estimates are unlikely to help you identify specific risks. Instead, you use activity cost estimates to help identify the risk of budget

Question

Which activities should you focus on when conducting a document analysis to identify project risks?

Options:

1. Looking for gaps or discrepancies among the inputs

2. Checking the quality of management plans

3. Examining all constraints and assumptions to identify associated risks

4. Performing an earned value analysis

5. Developing new risk templates

Answer

Option 1: This is a correct option. It's important to examine the inputs for problems such as gaps, contradictions, or other flaws that could represent risks.

Option 2: This is a correct option. The quality of the cost, schedule, and quality management plans is an important indicator of risk. Incomplete or vague plans create risk.

Option 3: This is a correct option. The constraints and assumptions in the project scope statement indicate risks and should be carefully reviewed.

Option 4: This is an incorrect option. Earned value analysis is not part of a documentation review to identify risk. However, earned value reports may be an input for risk identification once a project is in progress.

Option 5: This is an incorrect option. You would not develop risk templates during a documentation review, although you would review existing templates from previous projects. Creating new templates would be part of creating the risk management plan.

Option

If you're conducting a brainstorming session to identify project risks, which guidelines should you follow?

Options:

Risk Management Professional (PMBOK 6)

1. Involve participants from diverse backgrounds and areas of expertise
2. Define a specific objective for the session
3. Record all ideas
4. Encourage participants to build on each other's ideas
5. Invite suppliers and external experts to the brainstorming session
6. Select senior management only to participate

Answer

Option 1: This is a correct option. Input from a multidisciplinary group is required to ensure that risks in particular areas aren't overlooked.

Option 2: This is a correct option. Ensuring that you define a specific objective for the session allows you to identify and categorize certain risks.

Option 3: This is a correct option. Recording all the information ensures you do not lose any ideas.

Option 4: This is a correct option. Encouraging participants to build on each other's ideas allows you to identify, clarify, and categorize certain risks.

Option 5: This is an incorrect option. It would be inappropriate to include suppliers and external experts in the brainstorming session. Instead, interview these stakeholders separately to identify potential risks.

Option 6: This is an incorrect option. You should

involve stakeholders who have diverse backgrounds, viewpoints, and areas of expertise.

Question

When is the best time to use interviewing as a method for gathering risk information?

Options:

1. When brainstorming or other group sessions are not possible or appropriate
2. When assessing the merit of risks identified in a brainstorming session
3. When you need to analyze the groups of root causes that give rise to risks

Answer

Option 1: This is the correct option. It is inappropriate to include suppliers and external experts in the risk identification brainstorming session. Instead, you should interview these stakeholders to identify potential technical and regulatory risks.

Option 2: This is an incorrect option. All risks identified are worthy of merit. Interviews should be done when brainstorming or other group sessions are not possible or appropriate.

Option 3: This is an incorrect option. Although the cause of each risk should be identified where possible, root cause analysis – rather than simply a

Risk Management Professional (PMBOK 6) risk identification interview – is used to generate and analyze categories of risk sources.

Question

A company is racing to finish its newest products. The project manager identifies schedule delays as a major risk.

Match each possible cause of this risk to the cause category it falls into.

Options:

A. A breakdown in the scanning equipment used to track and manage shipments could result in delays

B. An insufficient number of vehicles ordered to transport the products

C. Inclement weather could delay deliveries for a number of days

Targets:

1. Physical
2. Human
3. Organizational

Answer

A malfunction in equipment or machinery is an example of a physical cause of risk.

Ordering an insufficient number of vehicles is an example of a human cause of error. Someone may miscalculate the size of the shipments or the required number of vehicles.

Bad weather is an external cause that impacts a project, making it an example of an organizational cause.

Question

You're managing a project to open a deli in a busy mall. You've done a SWOT analysis to help you identify the risks involved.

Match each factor to the area of the SWOT analysis it would fall in.

Options:

A. Good location

B. Little retail experience

C. Could expand into a chain

D. Subject to increases in costs of construction materials

Targets:

1. Strengths

2. Weaknesses

3. Opportunities

4. Threats

Answer

A good location for the deli – for example, in a busy shopping center – represents a strength. It's likely to contribute to the success of the project. This is an internal factor because it's one over which

Risk Management Professional (PMBOK 6) you can exert some control.

A lack of retail experience is a potential weakness that may compromise the success of the project. This is an internal factor that you could improve on.

If the deli is popular, there could be an opportunity to expand it into a chain. This is an external factor that depends on the way the public responds to the deli.

A possible threat to the project is price increases by construction material suppliers, which may force the project costs to increase greatly. This is a threat rather than a weakness because it's an external factor over which you have little control.

Question

What questions should a risk identification team ask about each project assumption or constraint during assumption and constraint analysis?

Options:

1. What impact would it have on the project if the assumption or constraint turned out to be false?

2. If the assumption or constraint proves to be false, what actions should be planned to limit the impact?

3. How valid is the assumption or constraint?

4. Who is responsible for having made the

assumption or constraint?

Answer

Option 1: This is a correct option. Knowing what effect a false assumption or constraint could have on the project is the only way to determine the level of risk it poses.

Option 2: This is an incorrect option. Assumptions and constraints analysis is a technique you use during the Identify Risks process. Generally, you complete this process before beginning to plan appropriate risk responses.

Option 3: This is a correct option. The team should check the validity of each assumption or constraint as an aspect of determining the risk it poses. This involves checking assumptions for accuracy, consistency, and completeness.

Option 4: This is an incorrect option. The issue of who was responsible for making particular assumptions or constraints is of little relevance for identifying or managing the risks they pose.

Question

Which documents can you gather information from when using checklists to identify risks?

Options:

1. The risk breakdown structure
2. The risk register from a similar past project

Risk Management Professional (PMBOK 6)

3. The work breakdown structure

4. The budgetary performance represented by the cost baselines of similar past projects

5. The project scope statement

Answer

Option 1: This is a correct option. The lowest levels of the risk breakdown structure are an excellent source for checklist items because they list potential risks that have already been identified for a project.

Option 2: This is a correct option. The risk register from a similar previous project can alert you to risks that will also affect the current project. It can also improve your understanding of these risks and guide the development of appropriate risk responses.

Option 3: This is an incorrect option. The work breakdown structure, or WBS, is a systematic decomposition of the deliverables needed to complete a project. The WBS is concerned with required activities rather than project risks.

Option 4: This is an incorrect option. Some of the most serious risks to your project may be linked to costs. However, the cost baselines and performance of past projects would not be a direct input for checklist analysis.

Option 5: This is an incorrect option. The project

scope statement provides an overview of what a project must achieve, but doesn't directly identify relevant risks or form an input for checklist analysis.

Question

Match sections in a risk register to examples of their content.

Options:

A. Risk
B. Impact
C. Cause
D. Response

Targets:

1. Delays in painting the external walls of the building
2. May miss deadline for task completion; potential overspend on budget
3. Bad weather delaying painting work
4. Adjust budget and increase number of workers to reduce delays

Answer

The risk section should clearly identify specific project risks such as delays in painting external walls in a construction or renovation project.

The impact section should describe the potential effects of each risk on the project, should the risk occur. For example, the impacts of delays could

Risk Management Professional (PMBOK 6) include missed deadlines and overspending.

The cause section lists the root causes of potential risks. In this case, bad weather could cause delays in painting external walls.

The response section may include accepting a risk if its cause lies outside of the management team's control and adjusting the project plan to accommodate its likely impact.

Question

Which elements are outputs of the Identify Risks process?

Options:

1. Lessons learned register updates
2. The risk register
3. The risk report
The assumptions log
5. Resource management plan updates

Answer

Option 1: This is a correct option. Updates to the lessons learned register, as well as other project documents such as the assumptions log and the issues log, are a typical output when identifying risks.

Option 2: This is a correct option. The risk register is a key document that describes each risk, its potential impact, and its root causes.

Option 3: This is a correct option. The risk report summarizes information related to the sources of project risk, threats and opportunities, and any specific risk metrics.

Option 4: This is an incorrect option. The assumptions log is an input to the Identify Risks process, not an output. However, during the process, you may need to update the assumptions log.

Option 5: This is an incorrect option. While the resource management plan is used as an input to the Identify Risks project, you do not usually make updates to it during the process.

3. Analyzing Risk (by PMBOK® Guide Sixth Edition)

3.1. Inputs to Perform Qualitative Risk Analysis
3.2. Qualitative Risk Analysis Tools and Techniques
3.3. Risk Probability and Impact Assessment
3.4. Outputs of Perform Qualitative Risk Analysis
3.5. Inputs to Perform Quantitative Risk Analysis
3.6. Gathering Quantitative Risk Data
3.7. Representing Uncertainty
3.8. Sensitivity Analysis for Quantitative Data
3.9. Decision Tree Analysis
3.10. Simulations
3.11. Risk Report Updates
3.12. Exercise: Analyzing Risk Data

3.1. Inputs to Perform Qualitative Risk Analysis

When you're managing a project, there are too many risks to worry about all of them. So the best approach is to analyze risks to determine which risks are the most likely to happen and which would have the greatest impact, and then prioritize them accordingly. That's the purpose of the perform qualitative risk analysis process.

As with all the processes in the risk management knowledge area, an important input to this process is the project management plan and any relevant subsidiary plans. In this process, the risk management plan information is necessary. The risk management plan identifies the roles and responsibilities of specific team members for managing risk. Generally, these individuals have the most knowledge about risks in their particular areas. So you use this information when you compile the list of attendees to the risk analysis meetings. [Risk analysis budget and schedule] The risk management budget states how much money is approved for risk management activities. The risk management schedule informs you of the amount of time available for risk management. You use the budget and the schedule to track the time and money spent on risk analysis.

Risk Management Professional (PMBOK 6)

Risk categories identify risk types such as technical, external, organizational, and those related to project management. Grouping risks like this enables you to determine where project risks are concentrated, so you can focus on those areas when you develop risk responses. [Definitions of probability and impact] Definitions of what constitutes low, medium, and high probability and impact are included in the risk management plan. These definitions help to minimize bias when prioritizing risks. [Stakeholders' risk tolerances] The less tolerance stakeholders have for risk, the more vigilant and aggressive you must be in the analyzing and responding to risk. It's important to keep your stakeholders' risk tolerance in mind as you analyze risks and make associated decisions. This helps ensure that risks are prioritized appropriately.

Another important input is relevant project documents. One of those documents you'll use is the risk register. It provides information about the risks that are to be analyzed, such as the cause, impact, severity rating, and likelihood of each risk. [It also provides information about tracking, RBS, WBS, date, description, and risk response.] The assumption log and stakeholder register are other important project documents you'll use as inputs to perform qualitative risk analysis.

Certain enterprise environmental factors act as an input and can provide insight and give context as you assess identified risks. Industry studies and risk databases often contain useful information. For example, say one of the risks on your project is related to the use of a new computer application by your development team. Some of the developers have questions about the stability and reliability of this software. Part of your risk analysis should involve researching consumer reviews by those in your industry who have used the product to see what others are saying about it.

And finally, organizational process assets are another input to the performed qualitative risk analysis process. Typically, the most useful asset will be historical information from completed projects that are similar to the one you are working on. This information can aid you in determining how to prioritize particular risks. For example, studying the previous project's risk register, you can find out which risks occurred and what their impact was. This helps you plan better risk management strategies for the current project.

So in summary, you use the perform qualitative risk analysis process to prioritize risks according to their probability and impact. The inputs to this

Risk Management Professional (PMBOK 6) process include the project management plan and subsidiary risk management plan. Project documents including the risk register, assumption log, and stakeholder register, enterprise environmental factors, and organizational process assets.

3.2. Qualitative Risk Analysis Tools and Techniques

There are seven different tools and techniques you can use to perform a qualitative risk analysis for your project. Expert judgment, data gathering, data analysis, interpersonal and team skills, risk categorization, data representation, and meetings.

You'll use expert judgment throughout your entire project. When it comes to performing qualitative risk analysis, you'll rely on the expert judgment of individuals and groups who have specialized training and knowledge of qualitative risk analysis.

A data gathering technique critical to performing a qualitative risk analysis is interviewing. You'll use interviews to gather the data you require for your analysis. For example, you'll need to find out how individual project risks could affect the project and the chances or probability of that happening by gaining insight from people who know that information.

And of course, along with that, you'll use another technique to perform qualitative risk analysis, interpersonal and team skills. One such skill is facilitation, which you use to keep participants focused on the task. Good facilitation also increases effectiveness of the analysis task as it

Risk Management Professional (PMBOK 6) involves helping participants to reach consensus, identifying and overcoming bias. Resolving any conflicts amongst participants, and guiding participants in the methods being used so the process is performed accurately.

Another technique you'll use, typically in combination with data gathering, is meetings. During the perform qualitative risk analysis process, the project team may hold risk workshops to discuss project risks. Specifically, to review identified risks and to assess, categorize, and prioritize risks.

Risk categorization is another technique useful in the qualitative risk analysis process. Risk categorization involves grouping sets of risks, for example, technical, external, and internal. This can reveal the areas of the project most exposed to risk and inform risk response planning. Here are the three most commonly used risk categories. First of all, you could categorize based on the sources of risk.

Categorizing risks based on their sources enables you to group them according to their root causes. This can help you plan effective risk responses. A useful tool for doing this is the risk breakdown structure. For example, the sources of quality related risks typically involve human error or technical error.

Grouping them under one heading may allow you to find a common response for controlling those risks, such as strengthening your quality control processes. Risks could be categorized by project area for analysis. The project's work breakdown structure contains project areas, so it is helpful to categorize risks according to the areas of the project they affect.

Each risk is linked to a specific work package. For example, the risk legal delays in land acquisition slots under the acquire land area. That may trigger the identification and analysis of other risks relating to acquiring land, such as protest from local residents.

If you choose to categorize risks according to a project's phases such as planning, development, monitoring, and closing phases, you link each risk to the project phase in which it's most likely to occur. For example, in a software development project, the risks that fall under the development phase may be failure to understand project scope or failure to account for staff shortages.

The next tool and technique is data analysis. Not that that should be a surprise considering what this process is about. There are a few different data analysis techniques particularly helpful in the perform qualitative risk analysis process. One is a

Risk Management Professional (PMBOK 6)
risk data quality assessment. If the information you and your team gather about identified risks is inaccurate, biased, or incomplete, the results of qualitative analysis will be unreliable.

There are three general criteria you should use to assess the quality of your risk data. The reliability of the data. For example, do you trust the source from which the data was gathered? The accuracy of the data and the relevance of the data to your project and its unique circumstances.

For example, are the conditions of the risk similar to those of the project from which the data was pulled? Each of those criteria help you determine the integrity of your data. If you determine that the quality of the data you have on hand is not sufficient to perform a thorough analysis, you may need to gather better quality data.

Another data analysis technique is a risk probability and impact assessment. This assessment method is used to determine the chances that a specific risk is going to occur in your project. For example, what are the chances a risk will impact the schedule, costs, quality, or performance?

And another data analysis method is performing an assessment of other risk parameters. Other risk characteristics besides probability and impact are urgency, proximity, dormancy, manageability, controllability, detectability, connectivity, strategic impact, and propinquity. It's a good idea to assess risks for any of these parameters if you think they may have an impact on your project.

For example, to assess how quickly each risk should be dealt with, the risk team uses the risk urgency assessment technique. This involves prioritizing risks based primarily on timing. Risks that could occur soon are seen as more urgent than those that may occur later on.

Other factors considered are the risks' probability and impact ratings. Risks with high ratings normally have a higher urgency and any warning signs that particular risks are likely to occur. You can rate risk timing as near-term, mid-term, or far-term risks based on how soon into a project they're likely to occur.

[Near-term risk] For example, a member of the quality assurance team identifies questionable work done by a particular contractor. This near-term risk must be dealt with immediately so that the contractor's remaining work meets requirements.

[Mid-term risk] Or a contractor is due to work on an area of the project in a few months. The risk of poor quality work by the contractor can be seen as a mid-term risk because although it can't be ignored, it doesn't require immediate attention.

Risk Management Professional (PMBOK 6)

[Far-term risk] Another example, if a project launched in late spring involves outdoor construction, a far-term risk may be delays due to winter weather conditions.

Data analysis techniques can help a risk management team organize risks based on the types of responses they may require. Ensure the accuracy of analysis results and prioritize risks according to how urgently they require attention.

The final technique of the perform qualitative risk analysis process is data representation. Data representation techniques allow you to visually represent the data you are analyzing.

Two methods of data representation are probability and impact matrices, which are grids you can use for mapping the probability of risks to its impacts. And hierarchical charts which are useful in situations where you are categorizing more than two parameters at a time.

3.3. Risk Probability and Impact Assessment

There are seven different tools and techniques you can use to perform a qualitative risk analysis for your project. Expert judgment, data gathering, data analysis, interpersonal and team skills, risk categorization, data representation and meetings. As you can imagine, data analysis is one of the most important aspects of this process. So for this topic, we're going to focus on one of the data analysis techniques you can use.

A risk probability and impact assessment. The purpose of this data analysis technique is to assign a combined probability impact rating to each risk identified for a project. You can then prioritize all risks based on the relative levels of threat or opportunity they represent. To conduct a risk probability and impact assessment, the risk planning team assesses risks either in a brainstorming session, interviews, or meetings. So you can see a few tools and techniques all coming together here. Expert judgment, interpersonal and team skills like facilitation, and meetings.

During the probability assessment, the team uses expert judgment to estimate how likely it is that each identified risk will occur, and the degree of impact the event would have if it did occur. To

Risk Management Professional (PMBOK 6)
ensure standard measures of probability are used across all risks, the team uses a scale defined in the risk management plan or one that is already available in the organization.

This scale may either be ordinal, which is low, medium and high, or cardinal, which would be a scale of 0 to 5 or 0 to 10. If you know enough about the probability, you may also assign the risk probability an actual percentage. To arrive at an overall risk score, you multiply its probability by its impact. So if you were using a low, medium, high type scale, you could use a chart similar to the one here to determine a risk's overall rating.

With quantitative risk analysis, you can use a probability and impact matrix. In this example, impact and probability have been given scores of 0 to 1. Let's address the probability first. A 0 would mean that there is no chance the risk will happen. While a 1 means that there is a 100% chance. A 0.5 would mean there's a 5% probability.

Each risk will be given a numerical value that falls somewhere along this scale. The project manager and team would work together and along with experts to assign the probabilities. Now, let's talk about impact. A 0 would mean that if the risk happens, it would have no effect on the project whatsoever. And a 1 would mean that the risk would impact the success or failure of the project completely.

Probability and impact by themselves aren't very helpful numbers. They must be used together to be meaningful. For instance, if a lottery jackpot is $2 million, you may focus only on the impact that money could have on your life. Why don't you run out and spend your entire paycheck on tickets?

Because you also consider the probability, and we all know that the odds of winning a lottery jackpot are very, very low. When we multiply the probability times the impact, we can determine the overall risk rating. This number is what we use to compare and rank risks. In this example matrix, the darkest squares represent high, the light gray squares represent medium, and the white squares represent low risk. So the darker the square the score falls into, the higher the overall risk rating is.

Let's use an example. Suppose you're developing a software user interface. You've identified a risk that the user interface will not adequately cover all of the needed privacy checks required by regulations. The risk has been assigned a probability of 0.3, which is low, but with an impact of 0.8, very high. When you align these two variables, the risk score is 0.24.

Referring to the sample probability and impact

Risk Management Professional (PMBOK 6)

matrix, a score of 0.24 is in the darkest range, which means it falls in the high risk category. If the risk assessment team uses a cardinal scale, each risk score has a numeric value.

This makes it even easier to place the risks in order of priority. For example, the list of risks provided here should be ordered with the customer changes risk at the top because it has a score 0.36. The inadequate user interface is next with a score of 0.32. And the final risk, prolonged lead times, is at the bottom with a score of 0.16.

If you're using ordinal values to rate probabilities and impacts, you can order the risks based on their associated priorities. The risks with the highest priorities are listed first. Prioritizing risks helps guide the planning of risk responses. For example, high priority threats may require aggressive response strategies. Whereas threats with low priority may simply be monitored. Similarly, high priority opportunities should be targeted first.

3.4. Outputs of Perform Qualitative Risk Analysis

The usefulness of the perform qualitative risk analysis process depends on the risk assessment team updating the appropriate project documents with the results of its analysis. These updates are the only output of the process.

One of the documents that may be updated as a result of risk analysis is the assumptions log. This is the place where you have recorded all of the project assumptions made during various planning and estimating processes.

Suppose one of the risks you had identified was the chance that a particular industry consultant scheduled to conduct product reviews would become unavailable during the review phase. As you are performing a risk data quality assessment, you realize the review activity duration and cost estimates are based on using this specific consultant. Since the assumption of availability represents a critical risk factor, you add it to the assumptions log.

One of the documents that gets most frequently updated as a result of this process is the risk register. During the identify risks process, the risk register is populated with a list of identified risks and information about them. After the perform qualitative risk analysis process, risk causes and

Risk Management Professional (PMBOK 6) categories may be updated.

There are other types of updates as well. After qualitative analysis, risks in the register are grouped by category based on their sources or the project areas or phases they're likely to affect. This can help identify common root causes of risks and simplifies the management of risks and risk responses.

Within each category the risks are listed according to their priority ratings as determined during the probability and impact assessment. The risk urgency assessment you conduct during the perform qualitative risk analysis process provides new information about which risks require the most immediate attention. So you update the risk register by marking near term risks as urgent.

Risks that require further analysis should be flagged in the register with symbols or color coding. For example, specific risks may be marked as requiring quantitative analysis after qualitative analysis has been completed. The risk register should already contain descriptions of risks and their causes. [A risk register displays.

The categories for all of the descriptions, which are late changes asked for by customer, user interface inadequately outlines regulations, and prolonged lead times construction tasks, are external.] These can be refined if more information becomes available during qualitative analysis. Additionally, new risk categories or newly identified risks may be added to the register. The causes of each risk are entered into the risk register during the identify risk process, however, if new details arise during qualitative analysis, these can be added to the existing descriptions.

For example, analysis may reveal that the risk of long lead times for construction tasks is due to possible strikes at the shipping stage. In addition to the assumption log and risk register, the other two project documents that typically get updated as a result of the perform qualitative risk analysis process, are the risk report and the issue log.

3.5. Inputs to Perform Quantitative Risk Analysis

During the perform qualitative risk analysis process, you asses project risks based on their probability and likely impact. In the performed quantitative risk analysis process, you take this a step further. You evaluate the risks in more detail and using more objective methods, so you can rate them numerically based on how they could affect overall project objectives. The perform quantitative risk analysis process relies on information from several inputs.

The first input is the project management plan which contains the risk management plan, scope baseline, Schedule baseline and cost baseline. The risk management plan details how project risk must be managed throughout a project, this information helps to determine whether quantitative analysis must occur, when it must occur and what form it must take It also identifies the budget available for risk analysis.

One way to measure the impact of a risk is in terms of how it will affect project costs and scope, for these reasons the cost baseline and scope baseline provide important information during quantitative risk analysis. And the information from the scope base line must be analyzed because many project risks are related to activity duration estimates and schedule over runs.

Another input to the perform quantitative risk analysis is project documents. There are many different project documents you'll use including the assumption log Basis of estimates, cost estimates, cost forecast, duration estimates, milestone list, resource requirements, risk register, risk report, and schedule forecasts.

The risk register is of particular importance as it identifies the project risks you need to analyze. And assign numeric values to during quantitative analysis. It also identifies risk categories and priorities. Often, quantitative analysis is performed only for risks that have been assigned priorities above a certain threshold value in the risk register.

And the last two inputs are organizational process assets, and enterprise environmental factors. Organizational process assets that can be useful inputs are risk related information about previous similar projects. Enterprise environmental factors can help provide context and insight into the environment in which the project work is being done. Two examples that may assist in risk analysis are industry studies of similar projects that have been conducted by risk specialists, and risk databases that contain information relevant to your

Risk Management Professional (PMBOK 6) project.

Let's walk through an example to see how some of the inputs maybe used. In a construction project the risk register identifies relevant risks their impact and severity and the likelihood that each risk will occur. [as well as their cause] Based on the budget and time available, the project management team decides to perform quantitative analysis only of risks marked as having high or very high severity.

The risk management plan specifies the techniques the team must use during the analysis. As well as when the analysis must occur. The team needs to measure the impacts of high severity risks based on how they could affect costs and the project deadlines. To do this, the team needs access to the budget, the cost plan And information about the project schedule. During quantitative analysis the team draws on organizational process assets like information from a previous similar construction project.

For instance late deliveries of building materials cause this project to miss important milestones Making it necessary to extend the project's schedule by eight days. This ultimately costs the project $140,000 in extra labor and equipment rental expenses. This information gives the team insight into how the risk of late deliveries could impact the current project.

There are several common questions you should ask when reviewing risk related historical information. What kinds of unplanned events occurred that cause a project's cost to escalate or deadlines to be missed? What strategies do the project team use to deal with the risks And were they successful, what were the financial impacts of particular risks? What were the schedule impacts of particular risks?

[In summary] The perform quantitative risk analysis process involves analyzing the effects of identified risks on project objective. And assigning numerical ratings to these risks based on their probability and impact. As inputs, the process relies on information from the project management plan, relevant project documents like the risk register, enterprise environmental factors and organizational process assets.

3.6. Gathering Quantitative Risk Data

Through the perform quantitative risk analysis process, you convert general information about project risks into concrete statistics. There are five different tools and techniques you can use for the perform quantitative risk analysis process. Expert judgment, data gathering, interpersonal and team skills, representations of uncertainty, and data analysis techniques. In this topic, we're going to focus on data gathering.

We're going to focus on the primary data gathering technique, interviewing. And we're also going to talk about expert judgment and facilitation, because they often work together.

Data gathering through interviews involves eliciting the information you need from experts who have it. The experts you interview may be members of the project team who have already played a role in qualitative risk analysis. Or they may be experts who have in-depth or specialized knowledge about the risks under consideration.

The main goal of an interview in this context is to collect data about the probability of achieving specific project objectives given the impacts of risks. For example, how likely is it that the project will finish exactly on time, and how likely is it that it will stay within the budget? For the purpose of quantitative analysis, the kind of information you'll be looking for to answer these questions is statistical in nature and usually expressed as percentages. For example, there may be a 50% chance of remaining within budget.

Another important area of information you need to gather is the assumptions behind the expert's opinion. You'll want to record the rationale for each estimate as an indication of the likely accuracy, sort of an ongoing risk data quality assessment. Usually the basic information you need to obtain from the interviewees is a three-point estimate of how each risk or risk category could affect a particular project objective.

For example, how much could the risk of bad weather affect the costs of a construction project given the best, most likely, and worst case scenarios? A three-point estimate is one that incorporates an optimistic or best case view, an estimate of what's most likely, and a pessimistic or worst case view of how events may unfold. As well as these estimates, it's important to record the rationale for them and any assumptions on which they're based. These provide insight about the reliability and accuracy of the estimates.

Let's look at an example, the project manager of

Risk Management Professional (PMBOK 6)
a banking software project interviews the lead programmer on the team to gather a three-point estimate of how long the phase may take to complete. After a discussion about how long each activity took on a similar past project, they determine that the best case scenario is 100 hours. The most likely is 120 hours and worst case would be 140 hours.

Based on the duration estimates, the project manager can determine the possible costs of the build phase. She has already estimated a rate of $1,500 for completing each hour of the work. Multiplying this rate by the time estimates for the phase gives a best case cost of $150,000, a most likely cost of $180,000, and a worst case cost of $210,000. She then takes the figure she has calculated to a group of experts to find out what they think the probabilities are that each estimate is accurate.

According to the experts, there's a 20% chance of the phase costing $150,000 to complete, that's the best case estimate. There's a 50% chance of the phase costing $180,000, which is the most likely. And a 30% chance of the phase costing $210,000, the worst case estimate.

For each estimate you would multiply the estimated dollar amount times the probability that was assigned by the experts, then you would add them all together. The sum of these amounts is $183,000, the budgeted amount for the build was $175,000, which is less than $183,000. Therefore, the budget should be increased. In the previous example, experts were able to assign actual percentages to the probability of the best, most likely, and worst scenarios.

If you weren't certain about the exact probabilities, don't worry, you can always utilize the PERT three- point estimate. With PERT you would simply weight the most likely scenario by four, and count the best case and worse case scenarios once each.

The best case estimate is that it will cost $150,000 to complete the phase of work. The most likely scenario is that it will cost $180,000. And the worst case estimate is that it will cost $210,000. In the numerator, you count the best case scenario once, the most likely estimate four times, and the worst case scenario is counted once.

The sum of these estimates is then divided by 6. If you're wondering why you divide by 6, it is because you use six estimates in the numerator. Remember, you counted the most likely scenario four times. When you calculate the three- point estimate using the PERT technique, the answer is

Risk Management Professional (PMBOK 6)

$180,000. That's pretty close to the estimate you arrived at when you used the experts.

While it's a technique you use throughout project management tasks, expert judgment is particularly useful for the perform quantitative risk analysis. Because you'll depend on the expertise of individuals and groups to wade through the information you'll gather. You'll count on expertise to determine the best modeling techniques to use, the most appropriate methods to represent uncertainty, and of course to interpret your results.

It's no surprise that since a lot of your activities for this process involve meeting with people to gather data, interacting with individuals or groups and consulting with experts, interpersonal and team skills are vital. For this process, facilitation skills are critical for effectively getting the information you need and managing the analysis work. Your facilitation skills are needed to establish and communicate the purpose of the work, garner trust and focus, keep people on task, build trust, and effectively manage any conflict or bias.

3.7. Representing Uncertainty

There are five different tools and techniques you can use for the perform quantitative risk analysis process. Expert judgment, data gathering, interpersonal and team skills, representations of uncertainty, and data analysis techniques. In this topic we're going to focus on representations of uncertainty.

Once you've gathered data about the statistical probabilities of risk, you need to represent individual project risks and other sources of uncertainty in a way you can utilize it.

Probability distributions are a method you can use for representing a range of possible values. A probability distribution is a graph that shows where the probabilities lie. The advantage of this type of graph is that it can depict a lot of information in one place, and in a format that's easy to interpret.

There are two main types of probability distributions. A discreet distribution includes the probabilities of a fixed number of outcomes. For example, represented in a bar chart. And a continuous distribution includes the probabilities of a full range of possible outcomes, usually represented as a curve.

Let's use an example. In a construction project,

Risk Management Professional (PMBOK 6)

you might use a discreet distribution to assess the probabilities of a task, like the installation of plumbing taking from four to nine days to complete. In a bar graph representing the distribution, separate bars show the probabilities for each of possible numbers of days. From this graph, you can deduce it's most probable that the task will take five or six days.

You would use a continuous distribution to show the probabilities of the possible costs of a project where these costs form an unbroken range. The curve in this example illustrates that most likely the total cost of a project will fall between 14 and $18 million.

If you would like to quantify the level of uncertainty, you may take the difference between the worst case scenario and best case scenario and divide by 6. In this case, you would subtract $14 million from $18 million to give you $4 million. When you divide by 6, the quantified amount of uncertainty is approximately $667,000. So you might say, this project will most likely cost $16 million +/- $667,000. This is just one example using a basic rule of thumb. Of course, the project manager and team may tailor estimation techniques as they see fit.

There are four common types of continuous

distribution, each with specific characteristics. The highest point in a normal distribution is the average value. All other values fall symmetrically on either side of this point to create a bell shape. A simple way of explaining this is that the further values move away from an average, the less likely they are to occur. The type of data you're dealing with will determine whether a normal distribution applies.

In a uniform distribution, all the possible outcomes between known upper and lower limits have the same probability. Think of rolling a six sided die, or reaching into a bag of colored candies where there's an equal number of each color. As you sample more and more, the distribution of your result should eventually be very uniform and equal across all the possibilities.

A beta distribution represents the probabilities of all values between specified minimum and maximum values. The most likely value is at the top of the curve. You determine the shape of the curve using mathematical methods. Beta may also be referred to as a skewed distribution.

In a triangular distribution, you plot only three values. Typically representing the best case, most likely and worst case scenarios. It's important to remember that the highest point in a triangular distribution isn't the same as the average value. It

Risk Management Professional (PMBOK 6) represents an expert's best guess. The average of the possible values may lie to the left or right of this point.

Each type of probability distribution is useful in particular circumstances. But the two type of distributions used most often in project risk analysis are beta and triangular distributions. [The Beta and Triangular distributions display.] Both are useful for representing the three-point estimates or best case, most likely, and worst case values that you establish during interviews.

Let's use an example to walk through creating a triangular distribution using risk data. For a software project, the manager interviewed experts to obtain a three point estimate of the possible cost of building the software.

The top point of the line in the graph lies at $200,000, which experts assign the highest probability of 50%. Experts determine there's a 20% chance of the software build phase costing $150,000.

And they determined a 30% chance of the phase costing $230,000. Using the triangular distribution, the project manager can now determine the probabilities of all possible costs for the phase in the range between 100,000 and $300,000. For example, there's roughly a 10% chance that the phase will cost only $135,000. There's also a 10% chance it will cost as much as $270,000.

In summary, to represent uncertainty, you use probability distributions. These may be discrete or continuous. Types of continuous distributions include normal, uniform, beta and triangular.

3.8. Sensitivity Analysis for Quantitative Data

There are five different tools and techniques you can use for the perform quantitative risk analysis process. Expert judgment, data gathering, interpersonal and team skills, representations of uncertainty and data analysis techniques. There are three different data analysis techniques that are particularly useful to perform quantitative risk analysis.

Simulations, sensitivity analysis, and decision tree analysis. In this topic, we're going to focus on the data analysis technique, sensitivity analysis. Sensitivity analysis involves testing how changes in one variable affect an outcome when all of the other variables are kept the same. By repeating the process for each of the variables one at a time, you can determine which of them has the greatest impact.

Consider a simple example, a spreadsheet lists estimated monthly expenses by type for a small administrative project. A formula automatically adds the expenses to calculate total monthly costs. You want to test the sensitivity of total costs if there is a change in the cost of renting office space. To do this, you can simply adjust the rental cost figure and check what effect this has on the total.

Sorin Dumitrascu

During risk data gathering interviews, you collect data about the probability and impact of risks. For instance, you may have determined the following about office rental costs. At best, rental cost will go up to $8,800 in January, in accordance with an agreed annual increase.

Most likely, a need for additional space will mean rental costs going up to $10,800. And at worst, a move to new premises may mean the rental costs go as high as $16,500. Based on the information you gathered, you can change the rental cost figure in the spreadsheet, while keeping all other figures the same.

This enables you to check the minimum, most likely, and maximum effect of the change on total costs. You can repeat the process to test how changes to each type of expense will affect total cost. This will tell you the types of expenses to which total costs are most sensitive.

In this example, the impact of a change to staff salaries is the greatest. So it poses the greatest risk, in terms of monthly cost objectives. A Tornado Diagram is a useful way to represent the results of a sensitivity analysis. In this type of diagram, a bar represents each risk and the range of the impact it could have, from negative to positive impact.

The length of each bar represents the relative

Risk Management Professional (PMBOK 6)

impact of each risk. The bars are ordered in sequence, from greatest impact to least. This gives the diagram its characteristic tornado shape. Many risks have potentially positive and negative impacts. For example, a cut in the size of a project team could mean reduced staffing costs, at the same time as posing a threat to the schedule.

A tornado diagram lets you determine whether the potential positive impact of a risk outweighs its potential negative impact. It also identifies risks in order of impact, so the team knows which risks pose the greatest threats or opportunities and so require the most focus. You can do risk analysis at the project level, as in this example, or you can analyze the effects if you isolate specific events or objectives.

In an Event-Oriented risk analysis, you assess how a specific risk event could impact the project. For example, this tornado diagram shows the effects on total project cost, if there was a 20% reduction in the number of staff working on the project. We can tell that the project would be most sensitive to any changes in the number of construction workers.

In summary, sensitivity analysis, one data analysis technique, involves testing the sensitivity of outcomes to one risk factor at a time. You can use it to rank project risks according to their potential

Sorin Dumitrascu

impacts.

3.9. Decision Tree Analysis

There are five different tools and techniques you can use for the perform quantitative risk analysis process. Expert judgment, data gathering, interpersonal and team skills, representations of uncertainty, and data analysis techniques. There are three different data analysis techniques that are particularly useful to perform quantitative risk analysis. Simulations, sensitivity analysis and decision tree analysis. In this topic, we're going to talk about the data analysis technique, decision tree analysis.

The importance of a risk to a project doesn't depend just on how much damage it could cause. It also depends on how likely it is that the risk will occur. This principle lies at the heart of decision tree analysis. It involves representing the choice between two or more options in the form of a diagram and using quantitative data to compare the possible outcomes of each of the options.

You do this by calculating the expected monetary value, or EMV. You use EMV analysis to determine the relative significance of risks, given both their possible impacts and their probabilities of occurring. To calculate the EMV of a risk, you multiply its potential impact by its probability. Say a risk could cost the project an extra $160,000, and this risk has a 22% or 0.22 probability of occurring. It has an expected monetary value of $35,200.

To perform decision tree analysis using EMV, you perform three steps. Determine the best case and worst case or optimistic and pessimistic EMVs for the first path and add them to get a total EMV for path 1. Do the same thing for path 2, then compare the two total EMVs to determine which option is best. One of the things you can use EMV analysis for is to compare the relative significance of different risks to help you prioritize them.

In this table, we've worked out the EMV for five risks. The one with the highest EMV is risk C. So it is the one that should have the highest priority when it comes to developing a risk response and regarding monitoring and control activities.

Another way you can use the EMV calculation is to develop realistic contingencies. If you add the potential cost of all the risks on this project, you reach a total of $2,248,000. But this assumes that every risk will occur and will have the worst possible impact. However, if you add up the EMVs for each risk, which gives a total EMV of $497,800. You get a much more plausible figure. Now you can draft a contingency budget based on probability.

You can use EMV calculation to evaluate the

Risk Management Professional (PMBOK 6)

impact of risks on the schedule, as well. For instance, at an EMV of 13.5, the risk of losing the lead architect poses the greatest threat to the schedule for this project, so it should have the highest priority. And if you total the impact times probability durations, the total delay you can expect if all the risks occur would be 32.15 days.

The best way to understand decision tree analysis is to walk through an example. In this example, we're going to compare the positive and negative outcomes of taking a specific action to determine whether that action should be taken. You're using decision tree analysis to determine if a change in your production process, removing a step, is worth making.

You label the decision node, remove step. You then add a path to represent the possible gains, cost savings due to efficiencies, and a path to represent the possible losses. Cost related to downtime and retooling. Next, you calculate the EMVs for the first path in the decision tree. There's a 30% chance that removing this step will save the project $10,000 for an EMV of $3,000.

A more pessimistic estimate is that there's a 70% chance that removing the step will save the project only $5,000. This gives an EMV of $3,500. The total EMV of path 1 is $6,500, which is the most probable amount the project will gain. Once you've completed adding values for the first path, you focus on the path representing the possible disadvantages of removing the step.

The optimistic EMV is a loss of $2,000. The worst case scenario for removing the step is a loss of $6,000. Together, the two EMVs give a total of -$8,000. Comparing the two total EMVs, we see that the expected costs outweigh expected gains. So the logical decision based on this analysis is to not remove the step in your production process.

In summary, expected monetary value or EMV analysis involves assessing risks in terms of both their estimated impact and probability. This can help you determine the likely significance of each of a set of risks. Decision tree analysis is often used as a specific application of EMV analysis. This involves representing the choice between two or more options and comparing the most probable outcomes of the options based on their total EMVs.

3.10. Simulations

There are five different tools and techniques you can use for the perform quantitative risk analysis process. Expert judgment, data gathering, interpersonal and team skills, representations of uncertainty, and data analysis techniques. There are three different data analysis techniques that are particularly useful to perform quantitative risk analysis. Simulations, sensitivity analysis, and decision tree analysis. In this topic, we're going to talk about simulations.

Sometimes the best way to find out is something will work, before you actually spend money creating it, is just simulate it. A simulation involves actually imitating a real system, so you can test how the system is likely to react given various conditions. If you can simulate project cost or the schedule, you can test how they will be affected by various risks.

There are two basic types of models, iterative and non-iterative. In an iterative model, the same what if scenario is played out repeatedly, each time with a different randomly chosen set of possible values for the variables that may affect its outcome. In theory, repeating the process many times gives this type of model the characteristic of accuracy.

The more times random values are chosen and used, the closer the model is to simulating random probability in real life.

In a non-iterative model, a single set of values representing the possible impacts and probabilities of each factor in an outcome, is used to determine a result. A widely used example of iterative modeling is Monte Carlo Simulation. Named after the famous Monte Carlo casino, it involves feeding data about the range of possible outcomes into a computer application. You can also weight this information.

For example, by specifying that values below an average are 20% more likely than values above the average. The system then repeatedly recalculates results, each time using values it chooses randomly from within the range you've specified.

Once the system has completed a very large number of calculations, it can provide statistics based on all the possible outcomes it has calculated. If you were to perform a simulation based risk analysis on the cost for a project, the required data for the Monte Carlo simulation is the cost estimates.

When schedule risks are the focus, you will require two sources of data. One is the duration estimates. The other source is the schedule network precedence diagram, which shows the tasks that must be completed, their sequence, and various

Risk Management Professional (PMBOK 6)

estimates of their durations. The result of this simulation is a prediction of how risks may impact cost or schedule objectives, usually in the form of a probability distribution.

Let's discuss an example of the results of a simulation and determine how we can use it to predict the likelihood of achieving specific targets. The project's target budget is $2.2 million. According to the line on the graph, there is only a 23% chance that the project will meet that target.

If the budget was $2.45 million, there is an 85% chance that the project would meet the cost target. If the risk management policy of the organization required a 75% likelihood that the project would meet its cost target, the budget would have to be increased to $2.4 million. These are just a few examples of how simulations can help you analyze risk data and make decisions that will help you better manage risks on your projects.

3.11. Risk Report Updates

Despite the amount of work you can imagine the perform quantitative risk analysis process requires, there's only one output of the process. Project document updates. And the project document typically updated is the risk report. You add the results of quantitative risk analysis to the risk report, so they can be used during the planning of appropriate risk responses.

The first type of information you will add to the risk report is the probabilistic analysis of the project. This provides statistics about the project's possible outcomes in terms of cost and time. Executive managers in your organization who authorize management reserves will be interested in the probabilistic analysis of the project. Through quantitative risk analysis, you've quantified the probability of achieving specific cost and schedule objectives.

So the results of assessing overall project risk exposure needs to be added to the risk report as well. Typically, you represent the probable total cost or duration of a project using a cumulative distribution. This type of graph lets you represent the probabilities of all possible outcomes using a single curve.

Risk Management Professional (PMBOK 6)

Similarly, you can use a probability distribution to represent the likelihood of achieving a specific project objective in terms of cost or the schedule. Based on the results of quantitative risk analysis, you re-prioritize the identified risks in each risk category, based on their possible impacts and their probabilities of occurring.

Ranking risks in this way tells the management team which risks it should prioritize when it plans risk responses. This information is then added to the risk report. Another type of information you should add to the risk report is any information about trends in the results of quantitative risk analysis. You can repeat quantitative risk analysis several times at different points in the project.

Trends or patterns that emerge in the results can guide the risk management team in prioritizing and addressing specific risks. Or point to the need for further risk analysis. For example, you may analyze cost-related risks before the start of each phase in a multi-phase project. And finally, you should include any recommended risk responses that you determine during your analysis activities.

In summary, the single output of the perform quantitative risk analysis process is project documents updates, which typically take the form of risk report updates. These updates include a probabilistic analysis of the project and assessment of the overall project risk exposure. A prioritized list of quantified risks, any trends in quantitative risk analysis results over time. And any recommended risk responses determined during the quantitative risk analysis.

3.12. Exercise: Analyzing Risk Data

In this exercise, you'll demonstrate your understanding of how to manage and mitigate the potential effects of risks on your project by carrying out different forms of analysis to assess their probability and impact.

In this exercise, you'll demonstrate that you can
1. recognize the inputs, tools and techniques, and outputs of the Perform Qualitative Risk Analysis process
2. recognize how to perform a risk probability and impact assessment
3. recognize the inputs, tools and techniques, and outputs of the Perform Quantitative Risk Analysis process
4. calculate the expected monetary value of a risk, and interpret a cost risk simulation graph

Question

What are the inputs to the Perform Qualitative Risk Analysis process?

Options:
1. Enterprise environmental factors
2. Stakeholder register
3. Organizational process assets

4. Risk management plan
5. Risk report
6. Durations estimates

Answer

Option 1: This is a correct option. Enterprise environmental factors to use as inputs to the Perform Qualitative Risk Analysis process are industry studies, risk databases, and consumer reviews.

Option 2: This is a correct option. The stakeholder register is a project document that is typically used when performing a qualitative risk analysis.

Option 3: This is a correct option. Organizational process assets, such as historical information from past projects, can help you plan risk management strategies for your current project.

Option 4: This is a correct option. The risk management plan is a subsidiary of the project management plan that outlines stakeholder roles and responsibilities, risk analysis budget and schedule, and risk categories.

Option 5: This is an incorrect option. The risk report is a project document, but it is not typically used as an input to the Perform Qualitative Risk Analysis process.

Option 6: This is an incorrect option. Duration

Risk Management Professional (PMBOK 6) estimates are usually used during the Perform Quantitative Risk Analysis process, not the Perform Qualitative Risk Analysis process.

Question

What are some of the tools and techniques you can use to perform qualitative risk analysis?

Options:

1. Meetings
2. Resource stacking
3. Expert judgment
4. Risk categorization
5. Assessment of risk parameters
6. Assumptions log
7. Hierarchical charts
8. Data gathering
9. Interpersonal and team skills

Answer

Option 1: This is a correct option. When carrying out a qualitative risk analysis, you may need to organize workshops with the project team to discuss, classify, and rate risks.

Option 2: This is an incorrect option. Resource stacking is a common response to project risk, but is not a technique used in the Perform Qualitative Risk Analysis process.

Option 3: This is a correct option. You may need

specialized expertise and advice in order to perform qualitative risk analysis effectively.

Option 4: This is a correct option. Risk categorization helps you analyze risks by grouping them together according to their sources.

Option 5: This is a correct option. Assessing risk parameters is a data analysis technique that enables you to gain different perspectives on identified risks.

Option 6: This is an incorrect option. The assumptions log is a project document that may be updated as a result of qualitative risk analysis, but is not a tool used during the process.

Option 7: This is a correct option. Hierarchical charts are one method of data representation that allow you to categorize more than two parameters at a time when performing a qualitative risk analysis.

Option 8: This is a correct option. Data gathering – specifically interviewing – is an important way of discovering individual risks that could affect your project.

Option 9: This is a correct option. In order to effectively manage interviews and team meetings, you'll need to have strong interpersonal skills, such as facilitation skills, to keep participants engaged in the tasks at hand and to resolve conflicts.

Risk Management Professional (PMBOK 6)

Question

You calculate priority scores for your project's risks:

- funding shortages: 0.06
- staffing shortages: 0.05
- loss of key personnel: 0.2
- resource problems: 0.28

Rank risk priorities from highest to lowest.

Options:

A. Resource problems
B. Loss of key personnel
C. Funding shortages
D. Staffing shortages

Answer

Resource problems is ranked

A risk priority rating of 0.28 ranks the resource problems risk as the highest priority risk in this case.

Loss of key personnel is ranked

A risk priority rating of 0.2 ranks the loss of key personnel risk as the second highest priority risk.

Funding shortages is ranked

A risk priority rating of 0.06 ranks the funding shortages risk as the third highest priority risk.

Staffing shortages is ranked

A risk priority rating of 0.05 ranks the staffing shortages risk as the fourth and lowest priority risk.

Question

Project document updates are the typical outputs of a qualitative risk analysis.

Which documents are updated?

Options:

1. Assumptions log
2. Risk register
3. Adjusted project budget
4. Adjusted project schedule
5. Risk report
6. Issue log

Answer

Option 1: This is a correct option. The assumptions log is one of the documents that may be updated as a result of risk analysis. In it, you record all the project assumptions made during various planning and estimating processes.

Option 2: This is a correct option. The risk register is one of the documents that may be updated as a result of risk analysis. It's an input to the Perform Quantitative Risk Analysis and Plan Risk Responses processes and is updated and adjusted throughout the project life cycle.

Option 3: This is an incorrect option. Adjusted project budgets are part of the project plan and are not updated after a qualitative risk analysis.

Risk Management Professional (PMBOK 6)

Option 4: This is an incorrect option. Adjusted project schedules are part of the project plan and are not updated after a qualitative risk analysis.

Option 5: This is a correct option. The risk report is one of the documents that may need to be updated as a result of risk analysis. It provides a summary of individual project risks and is also used as an input to the Perform Quantitative Risk Analysis process.

Option 6: This is a correct option. The issue log is a project document that might be updated as a result of risk analysis. It outlines problems that are currently affecting the project and measures to overcome them.

Question

What are the common inputs to the Perform Quantitative Risk Analysis process?

Options:

1. Scope baseline
2. Risk register
3. Historical information
4. Industry studies of similar projects
5. Resource management plan
6. The project charter

Answer

Option 1: This is a correct option. The scope

baseline is a part of the project management plan that outlines activity durations, which may be affected by potential risks.

Option 2: This is a correct option. An important project document, the risk register details project risks you need to analyze and assign numeric values to during quantitative risk analysis.

Option 3: This is a correct option. Historical information is an organizational process asset that enables you to discover what unplanned events and strategies were used in previous projects that may apply to your current one.

Option 4: This is a correct option. Enterprise environmental factors, like industry studies and risk databases, provide valuable insight when carrying out a quantitative risk analysis.

Option 5: This is an incorrect option. While the resource requirements document is a possible input to the Perform Quantitative Risk Analysis process, the resource management plan is not typically used.

Option 6: This is an incorrect option. The project charter may be an important input when planning risk management, but it is not used when carrying out a quantitative risk analysis.

Question

You're assessing the possible costs of

Risk Management Professional (PMBOK 6) completing an upgrade to your organization's network.

What are some of the examples of information you should obtain during a risk data gathering interview?

Options:

1. The lowest likely total cost of the project will be $280,000

2. The most likely total cost of the project will be in the region of $320,000

3. The total cost of the project could go as high as $450,000

4. The probability estimates are based on the costs of a previous similar network upgrade project, which faced comparable risks

5. A risk that could impact project costs is the possible incompatibility of the new network software with the older operating systems on some users' computers

6. The approved budget for the project is $310,000

Answer

Option 1: This is a correct option. During a risk data gathering interview, you should obtain a best-case estimate of what the project will cost, as well as likely cost and a worse-case estimate.

Option 2: This is a correct option. You should

obtain an estimate of what the project is most likely to cost, as well as best and worst-case estimates.

Option 3: This is a correct option. Part of the information you should gather is a worst-case estimate of how much the project could cost, given the risks it faces, as well as best-case and likely estimates.

Option 4: This is a correct option. As well as determining the best-case, most likely, and worst-case cost estimates, it's important to document the rationale on which these estimates are based.

Option 5: This is an incorrect option. You need to identify risks before using interviews to gather more data about them. This risk would affect the cost and time estimates for the project.

Option 6: This is an incorrect option. The approved budget amount isn't something you obtain by interviewing experts or stakeholders.

Question

What are the different types of continuous distribution?

Options:

1. Normal
2. Uniform
3. Beta
4. Triangular

Risk Management Professional (PMBOK 6)

5. Discrete
6. Bar graph

Answer

Option 1: This is a correct option. A normal distribution is symmetrical. The average value is at the top of the curve, and all other values fall evenly on either side to form a bell shape.

Option 2: This is a correct option. In a uniform distribution, each possible value within a given range is just as likely as any other. So in a graph, a straight line represents the distribution of probabilities.

Option 3: This is a correct option. A beta distribution includes a minimum and a maximum value, with a curve representing the probabilities of values in between. The highest point of the curve represents the most likely value.

Option 4: This is a correct option. A triangular distribution has a triangular shape because it connects three data points: best-case, most likely, and worst-case estimates. The peak of the triangle is near the top of the Y-axis scale.

Option 5: This is an incorrect option. A discrete distribution is one of the two types of probability distributions, the other being continuous.

Option 6: This is an incorrect option. Bar graphs are typically used to represent discrete distributions, not continuous distributions.

Question

What is the purpose of sensitivity analysis?

Options:

1. To determine which risks have the greatest potential impact

2. To identify which risks have the highest probability of occurring

3. To identify which risks may impact project objectives

4. To calculate the values of the positive versus negative impacts of the risk events

Answer

Option 1: This is the correct option. Sensitivity analysis involves identifying the relative potential impacts of different risks on project objectives. Based on the results, you can rank risks from greatest to least likely impact.

Option 2: This is an incorrect option. Sensitivity analysis doesn't identify the probabilities of different risks occurring. Rather, it identifies the relative potential impacts of risks on project objectives.

Option 3: This is an incorrect option. A risk management team typically identifies risks to a project before using either qualitative or quantitative

Risk Management Professional (PMBOK 6)

risk analysis to evaluate these risks.

Option 4: This is an incorrect option. The project management software you use would do the calculations. Sensitivity analysis is about identifying which risks have the greatest potential impact on project objectives.

Question

You determine that if new machinery is ordered, there's a 40% probability it will take 14 days to arrive and a 60% probability it will take 28 days.

What is the total EMV for ordering the machinery?

Options:
1. 22.4 days
2. 19.6 days
3. 11.2 days
4. 28 days

Answer

Option 1: This is the correct option. To calculate the EMV for a risk, you multiply its potential impact by its probability. In this case, you multiply 40% by 14 days and 60% by 28 days and add the totals together.

Option 2: This is an incorrect option. You've mixed up the probabilities. In this case, you would multiply 40% by 14 days and 60% by 28 days and then add the totals together to get an EMV of 22.4 days.

Option 3: This is an incorrect option. In order to establish the EMV for a risk, you multiply the potential impact by the probability. In this scenario, multiply 40% by 14 days and 60% by 28 days. Then add the totals together.

Option 4: This is an incorrect option. Multiply the potential impact by the probability to calculate the EMV for a risk. So in this case, you'd multiply 40% by 14 days and 60% by 28 days. Adding these totals together gives you total EMV – 22.4 days.

Question

The results of a cost risk simulation display on a cumulative chart.

Which statement describes what the highlighted point is communicating about the cost-related risk?

A cumulative chart of the total project cost contains an S-curve graph, with the X-axis labeled Cost and the Y-axis labeled Probability. The curve starts off at zero probability, then rises, before leveling off once it reaches 100%. The probability reading is 25% at the $43 million mark.

Options:

1. There is a 43% chance that the project will cost $25 million

Risk Management Professional (PMBOK 6)

2. If costs can be kept under $43 million, there is a 25% chance that the project will meet stakeholder expectations

3. There is a 25% chance that the project will meet a budget requirement of $43 million

4. Once expenses reach $43 million, 25% of the budget will be used up

Answer

Option 1: This is an incorrect option. According to the graph, the project has a 25% chance of costing $43 million.

Option 2: This is an incorrect option. The cumulative chart does not illustrate any relationship between budget and stakeholder expectations. Instead, it illustrates the likelihood of achieving specific cost targets.

Option 3: This is the correct option. The probability reading at the $43 million mark is 25%, indicating that the project has a 25% chance of costing $43 million.

Option 4: This is an incorrect option. The highlighted area actually indicates that the project has a 25% chance of costing $43 million.

Question

What information is generally updated in the risk report once the Perform Quantitative Risk Analysis process is completed?

Options:

1. The overall project risk exposure assessment
2. An in-depth probabilistic analysis of the project
3. A list of prioritized individual risks
4. Trends in quantitative risk analysis results
5. Recommended risk responses
6. Three-point cost estimates
7. A probability and impact matrix

Answer

Option 1: This is a correct option. The results of quantitative risk analysis include statistical probabilities of the outcomes of risks and of achieving cost and time objectives. Consequently, an evaluation of overall project risk exposure should be included.

Option 2: This is a correct option. An important output of quantitative risk analysis is a probabilistic analysis of the project, which shows how risks are most likely to impact a project's total cost and completion time. This information is often represented in the form of a cumulative distribution.

Option 3: This is a correct option. As a result of quantitative risk analysis, you can create a prioritized list of risks based on quantified data about their probable effects on a project. This

Risk Management Professional (PMBOK 6) provides an objective way for the risk management team to determine which risks to prioritize during risk response planning.

Option 4: This is a correct option. When you repeat quantitative risk analysis at different points in a project, trends – or patterns – may emerge in the analysis results. These can alert you to the likely effects of particular risks on the remainder of the project.

Option 5: This is a correct option. One of the main purposes of carrying out quantitative risk analysis is to provide feasible recommendations for responding to the risks highlighted.

Option 6: This is an incorrect option. Three-point cost estimates are an example of information you should gather about risks during an interview. These aren't typically included in the risk report.

Option 7: This is an incorrect option. A probability and impact matrix is a data representation tool used to perform a qualitative risk analysis, but is not included in the risk report.

4. Responding to Risk (by PMBOK® Guide Sixth Edition)

- 4.1. Inputs to Plan Risk Responses
- 4.2. Strategies for Negative Risks or Threats
- 4.3. Strategies for Positive Risks or Opportunities
- 4.4. Contingency Planning
- 4.5. Outputs of Plan Risk Responses
- 4.6. The Implement Risk Responses Process
- 4.7. Inputs to Monitor Risks
- 4.8. Risk Audits
- 4.9. Data Analysis for Monitoring Risks
- 4.10. Determining Appropriate Risk Responses
- 4.11. Outputs of Monitor Risks
- 4.12. Exercise: Planning and Responding to Risks

4.1. Inputs to Plan Risk Responses

In earthquake prone cities like Tokyo, you can't know if there will be a serious earthquake, when it will hit, or how much damage it will do. But this doesn't stop architects from designing tall buildings. They just incorporate the ability to withstand shocks.

Similarly, you can't know which risks will occur in a project, but you can plan how to best manage them if and when they do occur. The planned risk responses process involves determining the best possible responses to identified risks. Because there are several approaches you could take for dealing with risk, you need to select a strategy that will best support the objectives of your project.

There are four inputs in total to the plan risk responses process. The first we'll talk about is the project management plan, which includes three particularly helpful components for this process. The resource management plan, the risk management plan, and the cost baselines.

The resource management plan will guide you in coordinating resources for appropriate risk response activities. The risk management plan, which you create during the planned risk management process, introduces risk management and its purpose specific to the project at hand.

It gives an overview of the risk management approaches, tools, and sources of information that the management team must use to manage risk over the project life cycle. It contains the assumptions, constraints, and policies that relate to risk management.

Four components of the risk management plan [which are Roles and Responsibilities, Risk Analysis Definitions, Timing for Reviews, and Risk Thresholds.] are particularly useful in the plan risk responses process. The risk management plan outlines the roles and responsibilities of specific team members for managing risks. It can help identify team members with the most knowledge about particular risks.

These people can then be consulted during the planning of suitable risk responses. Risk analysis definitions in the risk management plan specify what criteria must be used to rate the probability, impact, and urgency of risks. This helps ensure that the ratings, which will inform the planned risk responses, are consistent and reliable.

The risk management plan outlines a schedule for risk management activities, including reviews of identified risks and their status. Planned risk responses may be altered based on these reviews.

Risk Management Professional (PMBOK 6)

The risk management plan defines risk thresholds for low, moderate, and high priority risks. These are the limits above which planned risk responses must be implemented.

For example, the plan might specify that once a risk results in a cost above $5,000, or a schedule delay longer than three days, the planned response must be put into action. During risk response planning, these thresholds help the team design specific responses for risks in each category. And the cost baseline component includes details about any allocated contingency funds for risk response.

The second input to the planned risk responses process are any relevant project documents. They include the lessons learned register, the project schedule, project team assignments, resource calendars, the risk register, risk report, and stakeholder register. As you can imagine, the risk register is vital. The risk register records all identified risks, and their severity, and probability ratings. It also includes information such as the root causes of risks, and their likely impact on the project.

The risk register also contains other information. Identifying risks that require immediate or near-term responses helps ensure that the team focuses on these risks early on in the plan risk responses process. Trends in qualitative risk analysis results can help the team identify patterns such as relationships between risks and their association with specific events. This information can help in the development of suitable responses.

It's useful to list low-priority risks that require monitoring rather than specific responses. It's also important to assign the responsibility for monitoring these risks to particular individuals. This helps ensure that if the priority of a risk increases, the team will know that an active response is required.

It's important to identify risks for which not enough information is currently available. This helps ensure the risks aren't forgotten. Once further analysis is complete, risk responses can be developed, or those already planned can be improved.

And the other two inputs are relevant enterprise environmental factors, or EEFs, and organizational process assets, or OPAs. EEFs relevant to the plan risk responses process include key stakeholder risk appetites and thresholds. OPAs that are relevant to the process can include risk management-related templates. For example, templates for the risk register and risk report, historical databases, and any available lessons learned repositories for past similar projects.

4.2. Strategies for Negative Risks or Threats

There are a total of nine different tools and techniques you can use to plan risk responses for your project. They include expert judgement, data gathering techniques such as interviews, interpersonal and team skills such as facilitation, strategies for threats, strategies for opportunities, contingent response strategies, and strategies for overall project risk.

You can also use data analysis techniques such as alternatives analysis and cost-benefit analysis. And decision-making techniques including multi-criteria decision analysis. In this topic, we're going to focus on strategies for threats.

You can think of threats as negative risks to your project. The main goal of the planned risk responses process is to identify the best strategies for managing project risks and there are five main strategies for managing negative risks. Escalate, avoid, transfer, mitigate and accept. In addition to risk response strategies, expert judgment, another tool and technique of the plan risk response process, is important when planning risk responses.

It may be provided by any group or person with specialized knowledge, skills, experience, or training in establishing risk responses. Occasionally, there may be a threat to your project that is beyond the scope of your authority as a project manager. We're not talking about typical project-related risks, we're talking about those curve balls that are responses required at the program, portfolio, or even executive level of the organization.

In these hopefully rare situations, your best response is to escalate the risk to the appropriate individual or group. Even though you aren't responsible for managing the risk, you still have a responsibility. You should determine who needs to know about the threat, communicate all important information about the threat, and ensure the appropriate individual or group accepts responsibility for managing the risk.

While the project team, including yourself as project manager, won't typically be involved in monitoring the risk any further. You should also record any relevant information in the risk register so the threat is documented. Let's review an example where escalation might be the best response.

You are the project manager for a new contact center to support end users of an electronic toll collection system. Which has been implemented to reduce traffic delays along a major highway. You receive a call from a representative of the local

Risk Management Professional (PMBOK 6)

media. The reporter wants you to give a statement about a lawsuit related to the toll rates along the highway.

You sense that answering this question would put you, your project and your organization at risk of negative media attention. And it doesn't feel right to comment about a current legal matter. Besides, the matter falls outside the scope of your project and your role as project manager. You refer the reporter to your internal legal or public relations department. Then you document the threat in the risk register. This would be an appropriate response in this situation.

Okay, let's talk about the avoid strategy. Sometimes negative risks are so costly or unpredictable that they should not be incurred at any cost. In this case, they must be avoided. In other words, planned risk responses must prevent the risks from affecting a project at all. Avoiding a risk can involve eliminating the cause of the risk, or it may involve changing the project management plan so that the risk isn't encountered.

In some cases, it can be appropriate to go as far as changing or relaxing a project objective that's in jeopardy. For example, say part of your production process was particularly complex and required highly trained and experienced workers. Instead of using in-house resources, you might choose to outsource that part of the process to an external vendor who specializes in it, thereby avoiding the risk of quality issues and delays.

Another strategy for threats is to transfer the risk. This involves shifting some or all of the negative risk to a third party. This doesn't remove the risk. It simply transfers responsibility for it to a party outside of the project. The strategy of transferring risk is most often used to manage financial risks. Most companies to which you can transfer financial risk have fairly high rates or fees for providing this service. So you should always consult the budget and perform a cost estimate before deciding to use this strategy. Examples of tools a project team may use to transfer negative risks are insurance and contracts that include penalties for breach of contract. Other examples are guarantees and warranties from suppliers.

Another strategy for responding to threats is to mitigate the risks. This involves reducing the probability that they'll occur and the impact they'll have if they do to acceptable levels. Let's look at some examples of techniques for mitigating risks. A project manager in charge of distributing charity funds realizes that errors in the printing, distribution and processing of application forms could result in the delayed or incorrect distribution of the funds.

To mitigate this risk, the project team develops an application form that can be accessed, completed and submitted online. Before a new computer game is released, the project team invites a target group to test a trial version of the game. Comments from members of the group are fed back to the design team, which then improves on the game. This mitigates the risk that the game will fail to satisfy consumers who buy it once it's released. If a product is at risk of late or unreliable deliveries from suppliers, choosing a reputable supplier with a proven track record can mitigate the risk. Problems with deliveries may still occur, but they're less likely.

Computer and network systems often include redundant features to mitigate the risk of system failures. For instance, one server may automatically take over the functions of another server that fails. Project managers often use this strategy of mitigating risks. And taking early action to reduce risks is much more effective than trying to repair the damage after they occur. However, mitigating risks doesn't eliminate them all together.

A fifth strategy for addressing negative risks is simply to accept the risks and their possible consequences. Acceptance is an appropriate strategy when a risk is small, unavoidable, unknown and can't be transferred, shared, or mitigated. In this case, a project team may simply hope for the best and plan to respond appropriately to any consequences or benefits that arise.

There are two kinds of acceptance, passive and active. Passive acceptance involves doing nothing unless a risk event occurs and then dealing with the consequences. Active acceptance involves accepting a risk, but planning beforehand how to deal with the consequences if the risk occurs. A common strategy is making sure enough reserves are set aside to put the plans in motion if they're needed. These are known as contingency reserves. They can be money or time.

So in summary, during risk response planning, strategies you may identify for responding to threats include escalating, avoiding, transferring, mitigating, or accepting negative risks. Or a combination of these strategies. In all cases, expert judgement should inform the choice of risk response strategies.

4.3. Strategies for Positive Risks or Opportunities

There are a total of nine different tools and techniques you can use to plan risk responses for your project. They include expert judgement, data gathering techniques, such as interviews, interpersonal and team skills such as facilitation, strategies for threats, strategies for opportunities, contingent response strategies and strategies for overall project risk.

You can also use data analysis techniques such as alternatives analysis and cost benefit analysis, and decision making techniques including multi-criteria decision analysis. In this topic, we're going to focus on strategies for opportunities or positive risks. In projects it's not only negative risks or threats that require planned responses. It can be just as important to plan how to respond to opportunities.

There are five different strategies you may decide on for responding to positive risks, Escalate, Exploit, Share, Enhance and Accept.

Occasionally, there may be an opportunity or positive risk beyond scope of your authority as a project manager. This would be an opportunity in which management and response is required at the program, portfolio, or even executive level of the organization.

In cases of positive risks of this nature, a suitable risk response is to escalate the risk to the appropriate individual or group. When escalation is your response, you still have a few responsibilities. First, you need to determine who needs to know about the opportunity. In other words, if it's beyond the scope of your authority, whose is it?

Once you've identified an appropriate risk owner, you need to communicate all important information about the opportunity, and also ensure the appropriate individual or group accepts responsibility for managing and responding to the positive risk. In addition, even though you and the rest of the project team aren't responsible for the risk once it's handed off, you should also record any relevant information about the opportunity in the risk register so the positive risk is documented.

Let's review an example where escalation is the most appropriate response. As a project manager, you often use a particular staffing vendor to provide skilled labor for your projects. The vendor brings to your attention that if you increase your orders by only 10%, you will qualify for a significant discount.

This discount would be very helpful in reducing staffing costs for your project. But your project

Risk Management Professional (PMBOK 6) cannot justify the increase in staffing necessary to qualify for the discount. You bring this offer to the attention of your human resources and procurement departments and document it in the risk register. Hopefully the decision will be made at a higher level to send more business to this vendor and receive the discount.

 To exploit a positive risk is to make the most of an opportunity by eliminating uncertainty in the project to ensure that it happens. This may involve changing a project's objectives, schedule, or budget. The project manager might achieve this by reducing the time period to complete a project by bringing in more qualified resources or by improving on the level of quality that was originally planned. For example, a training facility is in the process of launching a new business course. The project manager learns that a renowned lecturer and expert in the field has unexpectedly become available, and has expressed interest in the project. Having this individual involved with the project is likely to lead to an increase in enrollments, demand and profitability. To exploit this opportunity the budget will have to be increased. The objectives with regards to the course structure and layout may also have to be revised and altered. Exploiting an opportunity can be expensive in terms of cost, time, and other resources, so it's important to assess the benefits of exploiting an opportunity in relation to the expense of obtaining it.

While exploiting an opportunity involves trying to earn as much benefit from it as possible for a project, sometimes it can make more sense to share a risk. This involves joining with an external party to increase the chance of securing benefits and agreeing to share the rewards. For example, a manufacturing company wants to extend its sales into India. To minimize the risk, the project manager negotiates a partnership with an international marketing and distribution company that already has experience and an existing infrastructure in India.

Sharing the risk of entering the new market with this company improves the manufacturer's chance of success. The possible reward of going it alone would likely be larger but the risk of failing is much lower this way. Another risk response strategy is to enhance an opportunity. This involves taking steps to increase the likelihood or a positive impact of the opportunity on a project. For example, a casino may take active steps to win the approval of nearby residents by donating funds for local projects. This may enhance support for the casino and, in turn, increase the profits derived from local residents who may become regular casino visitors.

A final strategy for responding to positive risks is acceptance, especially in the case of an opportunity. It may be the best plan of action simply to accept the risk, don't take any action, and move on with the project. For example, a plumbing supply company has started supplying a major player in the building industry. The project manager for the account realizes that the company could secure further deals through the building contractor. However, being too pushy for additional business could annoy or scare off the client. So the manager decides it's best to continue providing good service and just to accept any extra contracts, should they come their way.

A decision flow diagram can help a team determine the best responses for positive risks. First of all, ensure that you have the authority to respond appropriately to the risk, if not, then escalate it. If you do, then you can determine the best response to it. If you can exploit an opportunity, you should do so. If not, then enhance it. If that's not possible, then share it. And if none of the approaches will work, you should accept it.

4.4. Contingency Planning

There are nine different tools and techniques you can use to plan risk responses for your project. They include expert judgement, data gathering techniques such as interviews, inter-personal and team skills such as facilitation. Strategies for threats, strategies for opportunities, contingent response strategies, and strategies for overall project risk.

You can also use data analysis techniques such as alternatives analysis and cost benefit analysis, and decision making techniques including multi-criteria decision analysis. This topic focuses on contingent response strategies. Also known as contingency planning, contingent response strategies involve assigning reserves so that the responses can be implemented when necessary.

Reserves are usually project funds but can include time, materials and staff. They are any resources needed to offset the impact a risk event has on a project's scope, schedule, cost, or quality. The level of risk for which you create contingency plans should depend largely on stakeholders' risk tolerance. The lower their risk tolerance, the more generous the contingency reserve should be.

It's important to monitor a project for impending risk events, so you can implement contingency

Risk Management Professional (PMBOK 6)

plans in time. To assist with monitoring, you can identify warning signs or triggers to watch out for. A trigger might be a threshold value of a performance metric such as cost performance, or a threshold defect rate.

Or it could be missing a milestone, or a change in a business relationship. Whatever the trigger, it should be clearly defined in the contingency plan and tracked during the project. An important part of contingency planning is setting aside enough reserves to put the planned responses in motion when risk events occur. But how big should the reserves you set aside be?

One method is to base contingency reserves on the expected monetary value, or EMV of the risk. To get the EMV, you multiply probability by the estimated impact in terms of cost or time. So for instance, if a risk has a 5% chance of occurring and the experts say it would likely cost your project $20,000, you'll multiply 0.05 by 20,000 and obtain an EMV of $1,000.

Some threats require time-based contingency plans. Including a contingency reserve in the schedule for a project helps ensure delays associated with risk events can be absorbed. To calculate the required schedule contingency reserve for a project, you use the EMV analysis method. But use time values rather than monetary values.

Suppose you take on an IT project to develop a database. You predict a 30% risk that you'll discover the project is more complex than you planned and this will add 40 days to the schedule. So you take 30% of 40, which is 12 days. You add a contingency of 12 days to the schedule.

In summary, using contingent response strategies or contingency planning, involves planning responses in case risk events occur and assigning reserves for implementing the responses.

4.5. Outputs of Plan Risk Responses

Imagine you're meeting with your project's primary investor. He asks you about the risk response strategy and you cannot answer his questions. Pushing the point, he demands to see the up to date risk register which you can't provide. As the meeting ends, he suggests that he may withdraw his funding of the project.

Business-savvy stakeholders will expect to see proof that the plan risk responses process has been applied properly. This proof is found in the outputs of the process, project management plan updates, project documents updates, and any necessary change requests as a result of planning risk responses. Most risks and responses have implications for a number of project management knowledge areas.

So the first output of the planned risk responses process is updates to the project management plan, including many of its specific subsidiary plans. Updates are typically necessary to the schedule management plan, cost management plan, quality management plan, and resource management plan. Procurement management plan, scope baseline, schedule baseline, and cost baseline. Updating these documents can be time consuming, but it is essential for keeping track of decisions throughout a project.

Relevant project documents updates are an output as well. This includes the assumption log, cost forecast, lessons learned register, project schedule, project team assignments, the risk register and the risk report.

Let's look at updates you might include for the risk register. The level of detail in the risk register should depend on a risk's type and priority, and on the nature of the response. For example, high and moderate impact risks should be addressed in detail. Lower priority risks should also be listed, but only for monitoring purposes. The risk register can contain various types of information to describe risks.

Tracking codes to associate each risk with the relevant components in the risk breakdown structure and work breakdown structure, [that is, RBS and WBS] the date of each entry, the category to which each risk belongs. For instance, planning or operational.

A description of each risk, for example, an operational risk is that critical path operations may be delayed. The cause or causes such as industrial relations disputes. Impacts such as that operations might be delayed for more than two weeks. The severity which in this case is high, and the

Risk Management Professional (PMBOK 6) probability of the risk which is moderate for this risk.

You add risk responses to the risk register as part of updating project documents. For instance, you record the planned risk response such as a plan to escalate, avoid, accept, mitigate, or transfer a risk or use a contingent response strategy.

You also record any action that will facilitate the response, or that will become necessary as a result of that response. In this case, you plan to accept the risk and note that if it occurs, the baseline schedule will be changed to accommodate delays. As well as adding planned responses to identified risks, it's important to update the risk register with residual and secondary risks and responses for managing them.

Residual risk is what remains after you've used a planned response to mitigate an identified risk as much as you can. The residual risk has a lower impact in priority than the original risk your response is designed to address. A secondary risk is a new risk that arises because of the planned response. Any risk response strategy can lead to one or more secondary risks.

Planning risk responses can also lead to change requests. It's not a guaranteed output, but as a result of planning risk responses, you may require change requests to the cost and schedule baselines or other project management plan components.

It's important to keep in mind that all the project risk management processes, including plan risk responses, are iterative in nature. This means that as new risks are identified, the processes are repeated. So you will likely find yourself planning new risk responses not only during the initial planning phase, but throughout your project life cycle.

In summary, the plan risk responses process includes three outputs. These are updates to the project management plan, and updates to other project documents and any necessary change requests.

4.6. The Implement Risk Responses Process

It probably feels like an incredible amount of time is spent on planning when you're managing a project, and it is. In fact almost half of all the project management processes are planning processes. And planning is essential, so you establish what you need, want, and work towards in reaching the goals of your project.

In terms of managing project risk, lots of effort is dedicated to identifying and analyzing risk. And also determining appropriate risk responses for the project. So what happens with all these great risk management plans? That's where the implement risk responses process comes in. Your proactive efforts in identifying, analyzing and determining valid responses for risks to your project are all great and worthwhile. But if none of them are implemented, what's the point?

The purpose of the implement risk responses process is to ensure that the agreed upon risk responses are actually executed. In other words, just like planning processes where you ensure appropriate planning efforts are made, in this process you are ensuring that appropriate efforts in executing the planned responses happens.

There are three inputs to the implement risk

responses process. The first input is the project management plan and any relevant components. For this process, the risk management plan is used. It contains details about project team and stakeholder risk management-related roles and responsibilities, which you use for assigning risk response owners. Other information included that you'll use is the risk management methodology level of detail and risk thresholds.

Another input includes any relevant project documents, including the lessons learned register, the risk register and the risk report. For example, the risk register will define the agreed upon risk responses along with the individuals or groups responsible for implementing the responses. And the last input includes any relevant organizational process assets. For example, the lessons learned repository may outline the effectiveness of risk responses that were used in other similar projects.

There are three key tools and techniques you can use to implement risk responses. Expert judgment, interpersonal and team skills, and a Project Management Information System, or PMIS.

Expert judgement can be that of yours or other experts with specialized training or knowledge in validating, modifying and determining how to best implement appropriate risk responses. The

Risk Management Professional (PMBOK 6)

implement risk responses process relies on your ability to encourage others to implement appropriate and agreed upon risk responses. Therefore, interpersonal and team skills, especially influencing, is critical.

The individuals or groups responsible for implementing risk responses may not be part of your project team. They could be risk owners outside the project team, or even outside the organization. Therefore the ability to convince risk owners to take on the necessary task at hand, even when they have other competing responsibilities, is essential. And a tool that will help you greatly to implement risk responses is a PMIS. Most PMIS include automated schedule, resource, and cost management features to help you store, retrieve, manage, track, and update relevant information.

There are two outputs of the implement risk responses process. First, you may have to issue change request as a result of the process. For example, a change may be necessary to the cost baseline, schedule baseline or a component of the project management plan. And any relevant project documents may need to be updated.

This includes the issue log, lessons learned register, project team assignments, the risk register and the risk report. For example, if an additional

Sorin Dumitrascu

response for a risk is necessary, this should be reflected in the risk register. And if the new response is managed by a different resource than originally identified, you should update the project team assignments for the risk accordingly.

4.7. Inputs to Monitor Risks

During the monitor risks process, you monitor warning signs that specific risks may occur, control risks using specified responses and identify and analyze new risks as they arise.

Project managers monitor risks for four main reasons. The first is to track risks and evaluate responses. As project work progresses, some risks may become more serious and others may disappear. To maintain an accurate picture of risk exposure, the project manager must track risks and the effectiveness of the planned responses in mitigating their impacts.

A project must be monitored so that new risks can be identified, analyzed, and planned for. Residual risks, or risks that remain after planned responses have been implemented, must be monitored to ensure they don't grow into more significant risks. Monitoring may indicate that the planned response for a risk isn't effective. In this case, contingency plans formulated during risk response planning should be implemented to control the risk. Now let's talk about the inputs to the monitor risks process.

There are four in total. First, we have the project management plan which includes the risk management plan. It identifies risk review processes, risk policies and procedures, reporting formats, and relevant roles and responsibilities for monitoring risk.

Another input is any relevant project documents. This includes the issue log, lessons learned register, risk register and risk report. For example, the risk register provides a wealth of information that's useful for monitoring risks. Let's talk about the risk register components that particularly inform how you monitor risks. Planned risk responses and specific actions for implementing them to minimize threats and capitalize on opportunities.

The triggers, symptoms, and warning signs that risk events have occurred or are about to occur. Residual and secondary risks, which may result from risk control activities and which require monitoring and control themselves, and time and cost contingency reserves.

The risk register also contains the impact thresholds for risks. If impacts exceed the stated thresholds, you activate the contingency plans. Thresholds may be set in terms of dollars, time, or resource limits, based on stakeholder's tolerance for risk. For example, if a deliverable is behind by 3 days, and the schedule tolerance is 5 days, a risk response will probably need to be activated.

Risk Management Professional (PMBOK 6)

The next input is work performance data. Here are some examples of work performance data that would be warning signals that a risk is about to occur or has already occurred. The current deliverable was completed in 68 days, which is 12 days later than planned.

The current schedule is at 45% complete, and it should be at 52%. Since there were very few errors in the code, the cost of testing the software was $2,700, which is less than the budgeted $3,000. Work performance data doesn't always reveal bad news. Remember that risks can be positive as well. You need to be vigilant watching for opportunities.

For example, schedule performance data may indicate that a phase is ahead of schedule because of unforeseen positive occurrences. That means the schedule contingency added to the phase is not needed and may be reallocated to high risk activities in a later phase of the project.

The final input, work performance reports, present work performance data that has been captured in previous processes. These reports may use various formats to convey project status. Bar charts and summary tables are two common formats for performance reports.

These reports provide information on variances, earned value and forecast. For example, they can outline planned and actual cost performance for each work package in a project. This helps project managers in monitoring risks and points to new risks that need analysis.

In summary, the monitor risks process is part of a monitoring and controlling process group. It is also the last process in the project risk management knowledge area. During this process, you monitor warning signs, activate risk responses, and identify new risks as they arise.

Inputs into this process include the project management plan, various project documents like the risk register, work performance data, and work performance reports.

4.8. Risk Audits

There are three tools and techniques that you can use for the monitor risks process. Data analysis techniques, which includes technical performance analysis and reserve analysis, audits and meetings. In this topic, we're going to focus on audits and meetings.

We're going to assume that meetings can be used with all of the other tools and techniques, in that you could perform any of them as a group. Risk management is something that should be done on a regular basis, every day, in fact.

During regular status meetings there should always be an agenda item to discuss project risks. The benefits of doing so are that risks are less likely to go unidentified or unmonitored. It also will help keep risk management as a discipline foremost in the mind of project team members and other stakeholders.

Audits are an effective technique to assess the effectiveness of risk management for your project. It occurs as project work progresses. During risk audits, either the project risk management team or an external auditor evaluates and documents the effectiveness of risk responses and risk management processes. The risk management plan specifies how often risk audits should occur, their objectives and the format they must take.

Following an audit, the project manager needs to decide how to respond and adjust risk response plans if necessary. For example, a software development team is holding their monthly risk audit meeting. One of the risks for the project is a potential shortage of programmers during the development phase. The team determines that the planned response to this risk, which was to add two additional programmers, is proving ineffective because they're still falling behind schedule.

They decide to adjust the response and look for three more programmers they can borrow from other projects in the company.

The depth and frequency of audits depends on a project's progress relative to its objectives. If the project is meeting its objectives, an audit doesn't need to be as vigorous as it would be if the project was in trouble.

Audits may be triggered whenever risk thresholds are exceeded. In the instance of the software project, the threshold for a certain risk is $1,000. So when the project manager notices a potential expenditure of $1,500 to address an issue, the company's risk auditing unit is called in to evaluate the effectiveness of the planned risk

Risk Management Professional (PMBOK 6) response.

When something like this happens, you should always remember to record the incident in the project's lessons learned register so that it will become part of the organization's lessons learned repository and can be used to prevent the same problem in future projects. Outcomes of audits can include changes to risk ratings, prioritization or responses. Or there may be no changes necessary if the audit reveals that risk management and responses are adequate.

4.9. Data Analysis for Monitoring Risks

There are three tools and techniques that you can use for the monitor risks process. Data analysis techniques, audits, and meetings. In this topic, we're going to talk about data analysis techniques.

The two data analysis techniques commonly used for monitoring risks are technical performance analysis and reserve analysis. Technical performance analysis focuses on product-related risks such as scope, functionality and quality. And compares actual and planned technical achievements in key performance areas. The success of technical performance analysis depends heavily on the team identifying the correct key performance parameters at the outset of a project.

Technical performance parameters include any quantifiable measures of its attributes, such as the product's features, size, speed, or output capacity. Weight, storage capacity, transaction times and number of delivered defects are all valid measurable criteria in technical performance analysis.

Reserve analysis involves comparing the remaining contingency reserves for a project with the remaining risks. This is to determine whether the reserves are sufficient to see you through to the end of the project. Throughout the execution of the

Risk Management Professional (PMBOK 6) project, some risks may occur with positive or negative impacts on the budget or schedule.

Reserve analysis protects the budget and schedule by ensuring contingency reserves are adequate to cover these impacts. Reserve analysis is also a good risk monitoring tool. Reserves that are too low could signify that a higher than expected number of risks have already occurred to drain reserves.

Measurable criteria and reserve analysis includes budget or cost and duration or schedule measures. The project manager monitors the project's performance over time by comparing actual performance and technical achievements to the product's specifications and quality parameters.

Set out in the product requirements documentation. Any variances point to a risk of the project failing to achieve its quality, scope, schedule and budget objectives.

For example, a website development project has a milestone for having the prototype running bug free by May 15th. A quality control report states the testing conducted on May 14th revealed 25 bugs that need to be fixed.

The project manager determines there is a high probability that the project will not make its final completion date. So the technical performance analysis technique helps project managers monitor the risk of failing to meet requirements and provides early warning of technical problems with the product.

4.10. Determining Appropriate Risk Responses

In the event of a risk issue, it might be helpful to follow a simple flow chart. By asking yourself a few simple questions, you can navigate through the proper steps. If a risk event occurs, the first question you might ask is, was the risk identified during risk planning?

If so, you already have a wealth of resources to address the risk starting with the risk register. You can consult the risk register and implement the planned risk response. If the risk event results in additional costs to the project, you've likely already allocated funds in your contingency reserves to be used for this very reason. However, if a risk event was unforeseen, this is a different scenario.

Think of it in terms of driving a car, lots of expected things happen, you're low on fuel, you drive to the gas station and fill up. You have a flat tire, you either change it yourself or call for roadside assistance. But what if you're driving along and an unfamiliar warning lights up on your instrument panel, what then? Well, it's likely you'll pull over, open the glove box, and check the owner's manual. Your project works the same exact way.

If you encounter an unknown, unknown, or a risk you didn't account for, you consult the owner's manual for your project. The project management plan, or more specifically, the risk management plan. Any cost will come from management reserves, and you will make the appropriate document updates to immediately incorporate lessons learned. And submit necessary change requests. Following this simple flow chart should help make things easier as risk events happen in your project.

4.11. Outputs of Monitor Risks

The results of the monitor risks process are produced continuously and contribute to a project team's evolving knowledge and understanding of risks until a project reaches a close.

The monitor risks process has five outputs. They are work performance information, change requests, project management plan updates, project documents updates, and organizational process assets updates.

The work performance data that acted as an input to the monitor risks process becomes work performance information after the tools and techniques are applied to it. This information, such as earned value measurements and forecasts, is what you communicate to stakeholders and use to make good risk management decisions.

The monitor risks process may result in change requests if risk monitoring activities involve changes to the project management plan or project baselines. For example, a new risk is identified part way through your project. Altering a certain process will allow you to avoid the risk. You create a change request to revise the work instructions for the activity and the corresponding areas of the scope baseline that would be impacted.

Sorin Dumitrascu

Change requests generated during the monitor risks process take the form of either corrective action for a risk that has occurred or preventive action for a risk that is likely to occur. Corrective actions include implementing contingency plans and workaround plans. A contingency plan is a provision in the project management plan that specifies how a risk will be handled if that risk occurs. Specific money or time reserves may be allocated for implementing the plan. A workaround is an unplanned and quick response to a negative risk that has occurred.

Preventive actions are steps taken to prevent risks from threatening project objectives. For example, if there is a risk that a specific work package will not be completed on time, a change request can be submitted asking for an increase in the budget to assign more resources to the task.

When change requests are granted, you need to update the project management plan with new information. For example, say your request for more resources is granted. You'll need to update the cost baseline, the resource management plan, and any other components of the project management plan that would be impacted by the change.

Project documents updates are also an output. These may include updates to the assumption log,

Risk Management Professional (PMBOK 6)
issue log, lessons learned register, risk register, and risk report.

Certain organizational process assets may also require an update as a result of the monitor risks process. Some examples are the risk breakdown structure, and templates for the risk management plan, risk register, risk report and probability and impact matrix.

4.12. Exercise: Planning and Responding to Risks
Exercise Overview

In this exercise, you'll demonstrate your understanding of how to successfully manage risks to your project by planning effective risk responses that will prevent or mitigate them, and by executing responses as needed, monitoring risk events as they occur, and identifying any new risks that may arise throughout your project.

In this exercise, you'll demonstrate that you can
- identify strategies for responding to positive or negative risks,
- recognize the inputs, tools and techniques, and outputs of the Plan Risk Responses process,
- recognize the inputs, tools and techniques, and outputs of the Implement Risk Responses process,
- recognize the inputs, tools and techniques, and outputs of the Monitor Risks process, and
- identify appropriate risk responses in a given scenario.

Question
What are some of the inputs to the Plan Risk

Risk Management Professional (PMBOK 6) Responses process?

Options:

1. The risk management plan
2. The project schedule
3. Stakeholder risk appetites and thresholds
4. Lessons learned repositories from past similar projects
5. Work performance reports
6. Contingency plans

Answer

Option 1: This is a correct option. The risk management plan is a component of the project management plan that outlines risk management methods, tools, and sources of information that can be used to develop responses to risks.

Option 2: This is a correct option. The project schedule, which is a project document, details activity durations which may be useful for planning risk responses.

Option 3: This is a correct option. The degree to which key stakeholders are willing to accept and tolerate certain risks is an enterprise environmental factor you should take into account during the Plan Risk Responses process.

Option 4: This is a correct option. Lessons learned from previous projects is one of the organizational process assets that you can take advantage of to help you plan risk responses.

Option 5: This is an incorrect option. Work performance reports are an input to the Monitor Risk process, not the Plan Risk Response process.

Option 6: This is an incorrect option. Contingency plans are a type of change request that are one of the outputs of the Monitor Risks process.

Question

Which strategies can be used to respond to negative risks?

Options:

1. Avoid
2. Transfer
3. Mitigate
4. Accept
5. Share
6. Exploit
7. Escalate

Answer

Option 1: This is a correct option. Some risks are so costly or unpredictable that they should not be incurred; they must be avoided at any cost. Planned risk responses must prevent the risks from affecting the project at all.

Option 2: This is a correct option. The strategy to transfer risk involves shifting some or all of a ns to a third party. This doesn't remove the risk, but rather transfers responsibility for the risk to a party outside of the project.

Option 3: This is a correct option. The strategy to mitigate risks involves reducing the probability that they'll occur and the impact they'll have if they do to acceptable levels.

Option 4: This is a correct option. The strategy of active or passive acceptance is appropriate when a risk is small, unavoidable, or unknown and can't be transferred, shared, or mitigated.

Option 5: This is an incorrect option. Sharing as a risk response is a strategy applicable to positive risks.

Option 6: This is an incorrect option. Exploiting as a risk response is a strategy applicable to positive risks.

Option 7: This is a correct option. The strategy of escalation is appropriate when you identify a risk that doesn't affect your project but may have a negative impact somewhere else in your organization.

Question

Which strategies are available for responding to positive risks?

Options:

1. Exploiting
2. Sharing
3. Enhancing
4. Accepting
5. Mitigating
6. Avoiding
7. Escalating

Answer

Option 1: This is a correct option. Exploiting an opportunity involves trying to earn as much benefit from it as possible for a project.

Option 2: This is a correct option. Sharing a risk involves joining with an external party to increase the chance of securing benefits and agreeing to share the rewards.

Option 3: This is a correct option. The risk response strategy of enhancing an opportunity involves taking steps to increase the opportunity's likelihood or positive impact on a project.

Option 4: This is a correct option. This particular risk response strategy involves acknowledging a risk but not preparing a particular response to share, exploit, or enhance it.

Option 5: This is an incorrect option. Mitigation as a risk response is a strategy applicable to negative risks.

Option 6: This is an incorrect option. Avoidance

Risk Management Professional (PMBOK 6)

as a risk response is a strategy applicable to negative risks.

Option 7: This is a correct option. This strategy is appropriate when a potential risk doesn't affect your project but may be useful for someone else in the organization.

Question

A supplier for a project has the lowest costs. However, there's a risk they could go out of business during the project.

Which risk response is the appropriate use of a contingent response strategy?

Options:

1. You create a plan, with budgetary and time reserves, for buying materials from the next preferred supplier on the list, although this supplier is more expensive and takes longer to deliver

2. You accept the risk and plan to respond to it based on how it affects project objectives

3. You try to transfer the risk to the supplier, which is facing bankruptcy, by insisting that this supplier honor the supply contract

4. At the start of the project, you submit a request to change the product scope by switching to a material that is available from a number of lower-quality suppliers

Answer

Option 1: This is the correct option. By developing a plan and allocating reserves, you ensure you can respond appropriately if the risk of losing a key supplier actually occurs. This is an example of an appropriate contingent response strategy.

Option 2: This is an incorrect option. Simply accepting the risk, without defining a clear plan or allocating reserves to cover it, isn't an example of a contingent response strategy.

Option 3: This is an incorrect option. This response does not indicate that you've developed a sensible contingency plan or set aside any reserves to handle the risk.

Option 4: This is an incorrect option. The response in this example involves an attempt to mitigate the risk by reducing the likelihood that it will occur. A contingent response strategy would involve planning and assigning reserves for handling the risk only once it occurs.

Question

What are typical outputs of the Plan Risk Responses process?

Options:

1. Resource management plan updates

Risk Management Professional (PMBOK 6)

2. Change requests
3. Updates to the assumption log
4. Scope baseline updates
5. Cost forecast updates
6. Risk management-related templates
7. Work performance information

Answer

Option 1: This is a correct option. An accelerated schedule, for example, may mean extra team members will be needed. Some team members will have to take on additional roles, and this information must be detailed in the project management plan – specifically the resource management plan.

Option 2: This is a correct option. Change requests are not a certain output of the Plan Risk Responses process, but may be required if, for example, cost and schedule baselines need to be updated.

Option 3: This is a correct option. Planning risk responses can lead to updates to the assumption log, which is a key project document.

Option 4: This is a correct option. The scope baseline, a component of the project management plan, will have to be updated if the risk response plan is triggered because the response involves eliminating the most time-consuming activities from the project.

Option 5: This is a correct option. Cost forecasts are project documents that may need to be updated depending on the risk responses that are developed.

Option 6: This is an incorrect option. Risk management-related templates are organizational process assets used as an input to the Plan Risk Responses process, not an output.

Option 7: This is an incorrect option. Work performance information is one of the outputs of the Monitor Risks process, not the Plan Risk Responses process.

Question

What is the key purpose of the Implement Risk Responses process?

Options:

1. To ensure that approved planned risk responses are carried out

2. To ensure that responses to all identified risks are developed

3. To ensure that the probability and impact of risks are analyzed effectively

4. To ensure that the consequences of risk events are closely monitored

Answer

Option 1: This is the correct option. Once you've

Risk Management Professional (PMBOK 6) analyzed all the potential risks and determined appropriate responses to those risks, the next step is to ensure that designated stakeholders make the necessary efforts in carrying out the planned responses.

Option 2: This is an incorrect option. This is the purpose of the Plan Risk Responses process, not the Implement Risk Responses process.

Option 3: This is an incorrect option. Ensuring that risks are effectively analyzed is the aim of the Perform Qualitative Risk Analysis and Perform Quantitative Risk Analysis processes.

Option 4: This is an incorrect option. This is the objective of the Monitor Risks process, which usually follows the Implement Risk Responses process.

Question

What are some common inputs to the Monitor Risks process?

Options:
1. The risk register
2. The risk management plan
3. Work performance reports
4. Work performance data
5. Updates to risk ratings
6. The assumption log

Answer

Option 1: This is a correct option. The risk register outlines planned risk responses, risk triggers, contingency reserves, and impact thresholds.

Option 2: This is a correct option. Typical information included in the risk management plan is risk review processes, risk policies and procedures, and reporting formats.

Option 3: This is a correct option. Work performance reports illustrate project status and provide information on variances, earned value, and forecasts.

Option 4: This is a correct option. Work performance data that can be used as inputs to the Monitor Risks process include warning signs such as the deliverable status, schedule progress, and actual costs.

Option 5: This is an incorrect option. Changes to risk ratings are typically the result of risk audits, and are not an input when monitoring risks.

Option 6: This is an incorrect option. The assumption log is created early on in the project management life cycle. However, updates to the assumption log are commonly an output of the Monitor Risks process.

Risk Management Professional (PMBOK 6)

Question

What are correct examples of risk audits?

Options:

1. An increased risk of lumber shortages is brought to the project manager's attention and the response to the risk is adjusted accordingly

2. A third party certifies that the project team's responses to pilferage risks are adequate and cost efficient

3. During a meeting, a team member notes that the risk of late materials delivery is no longer relevant

4. An S-curve reveals that project spending is in line with the cost performance baseline

5. Comparing current with past schedule data reveals that retooling is ahead of schedule

Answer

Option 1: This is a correct option. In risk audits, new risks are identified and responses are developed for them. Risk audits also work to ensure that risk responses remain adequate.

Option 2: This is a correct option. Audits are often performed by outside personnel who are trained in audit techniques. The purpose of a risk audit is to identify risk responses that are inadequate and any areas where new responses are required.

Option 3: This is a correct option. Risk audits

typically occur through risk status meetings. Audits help ensure that risk responses remain adequate and that both new risks and risks that no longer apply are identified.

Option 4: This is an incorrect option. This is actually an example of variance analysis, which evaluates the differences between planned and actual performance in terms of costs, schedule, or other performance criteria.

Option 5: This is an incorrect option. This is actually an example of trend analysis, which evaluates performance by focusing on identifying patterns over time.

Question

Match the technical performance analysis and reserve analysis measurement criteria to the data analysis techniques they apply to. Techniques may have more than one match.

Options:

A. Storage capacity
B. Transaction times
C. Number of delivered defects
D. Budget
E. Schedule

Targets:

1. Technical performance analysis
2. Reserve analysis

Risk Management Professional (PMBOK 6)

Answer

Technical performance analysis examines scope, functionality, and quality risks associated with a product. Valid measurable criteria when carrying out a technical performance analysis include storage capacity, transaction times, and number of delivered defects. Another quantifiable measure is a product's weight.

Reserve analysis examines whether the buffers put in place to account for certain risks are sufficient to help you mitigate those risks and complete a project. Criteria used in reserve analysis are budget and schedule measures.

Question

Match the risk response strategies to the corresponding risk events. More than one strategy may match to each risk event.

Options:

A. Consult the risk register and implement the planned risk response

B. Use management reserves

C. Consult the risk management plan

D. Update relevant project documents and submit change requests if necessary E. Use contingency reserves

Targets:

1. A currency exchange rate suddenly and unexpectedly spikes, increasing the costs of imported equipment needed for your project

2. New health regulations, which had been expected, are implemented, affecting the development of a new drug

Answer

For unforeseen risk events, you should review the risk management plan and take any costs incurred as a result of mitigating the impact of the event from management reserves.

As this risk was previously identified, it should already be detailed in the risk register and have a planned risk response. Once this is implemented, you then update any relevant project documents, submit the necessary change requests, and take any additional costs from your project's contingency reserves.

Question

Which outputs are typical of the Monitor Risks process?

Options:

1. The assumptions log is updated when you find out a designer will be available a week earlier than expected

2. The results of risk response audits are

Risk Management Professional (PMBOK 6)

recorded in the lessons learned database

3. A lead programmer e-mails you that his current task will be completed by the end of the day

4. The risk register indicates that a top priority risk is an impending strike at the production plant

5. The schedule baseline is updated when a risk is audited and found to require additional response time 6. You issue a change request to increase a budget to add more resources to an activity that may be delayed

7. Earned value is reassessed after a workaround is used

Answer

Option 1: This is a correct option. The assumption log is an example of a project document you may update based on the results of controlling risks. If an assumption changes, it should be updated in the document so that associated risks can be correctly identified.

Option 2: This is a correct option. The lessons learned database is an example of an organizational process asset. It should be updated with information and insights gained through monitoring project risks.

Option 3: This is an incorrect option. This would be an example of work performance data, which is an input to the Monitor Risks process, not an output.

Option 4: This is an incorrect option. Contents of the risk register are not examples of outputs of the Monitor Risks process. However, if details about an item in the risk register were updated as a result of controlling risks, that would be an example of a project document update.

Option 5: This is a correct option. The schedule baseline is a component of the project management plan that may be updated as a result of new information from monitoring specific risks.

Option 6: This is a correct option. A change request, such as the preventative action in this example, is one possible output of the Monitor Risks process.

Option 7: This is a correct option. Earned value measurements are a type of work performance information that result from analyses carried out during the Monitor Risks process.

www.ingramcontent.com/pod-product-compliance
Lightning Source LLC
Chambersburg PA
CBHW031618210526
45464CB00004B/1638